## DATE DUE

| | | | |
|---|---|---|---|
| | | | |
| | | | |
| | | | |
| | | | |
| | | | |
| | | | |
| | | | |
| | | | |
| | | | |
| | | | |
| | | | |
| | | | |
| | | | |
| | | | |
| | | | |
| | | | |

#47-0108 Peel Off Pressure Sensitive

*Dance — An Art in Academe*

# Dance
## An Art in Academe

Edited by

MARTIN HABERMAN
TOBIE GARTH MEISEL

*Teachers College Press*
Teachers College, Columbia University
New York, New York

© 1970 by Teachers College, Columbia University
Library of Congress Catalog Card Number: 70-108839

Manufactured in the United States of America

*For*

*MICHAEL*

*And Others Who Would Dance*

# Contents

# Editors' Preface

Lately it seems the arts are everybody's bag. And dance in particular attracts a polyglot following, ranging from the legitimate artist to the educator, physiotherapist, psychotherapist, social scientist, body awareness enthusiast, and the "Pepsi generation." As a result of this receptive climate, many organizations devote massive resources to programs in the arts. Having worked in dance for one such organization, we saw the need and opportunity for compiling this book.

We have attempted to acquaint the reader with the ideas and efforts of certain productive people, many of whom have been too busy heretofore to describe their work in writing. Our purpose is to bring discussions on the nature of dance and its place in education closer to the point where action can be taken—more real programs begun, more real children taught. It has been our experience that academic debate over well-worn issues does not lead to any real change. The issues we have raised are not shopworn. They are critical considerations for the artist and the educator attempting realistic change in the schools. The obvious choice is either to accept some of the positions outlined in this book as guidelines for changing practices, or to develop other alternatives. We are certain that if dance is to be considered an integral part of society and education, these issues must be contended with now. With the current wave of renewed interest in the arts, this is the time to act.

Since dance is part of every society's culture, its function is to both reflect and shape that society; the role of the school is supposedly the same. Acting as middlemen between artists and educators is difficult. Both groups are unclear as to the place of dance in education. Some artists feel that dance has no place in the school because the integrity of the art would not survive an institutional atmosphere. Others feel that getting dance into the school is an amendment long overdue, and they differ only in terms of instructional personnel

and practices. At the university level there is often an artificial distinction between the scholar and the performer. Now is the time for real change to be
effected, since groups within the dance community are seeking to clarify their
positions and educators seem more readily disposed to consider dance a legitimate field of study.

Our basic assumption is that dance has intrinsic value for all. Not only can
it be an instrumentality for improving mental health, physical coordination,
self-concept and the like, but it is an art form which provides a unique opportunity for expression of man's natural aesthetic sense.

This book deals with dance as a legitimate art form and explains its rightful
place in education. It is intended that serious students deepen their understanding of dance on the basis of opinions and perceptions of experts in dance
and related fields. At the same time, it is important to us that curriculum developers, educators, and other decision makers understand both the art of
dance and the need for dance in the school.

While the contributions we have selected must, by implication, reflect our own
position, the reader will nevertheless encounter honest and forceful discussion
of many conflicting viewpoints. The fact that these outstanding specialists
have seen the need and written the material we outlined ought to convince
someone that it is time to do something about dance in education.

We gratefully acknowledge the assistance of Sarah Patton and Bonnie Ken-
nedy in preparing the manuscript, and extend warm thanks to the many dedicated dancers who not only gave us a vision but were willing to help us learn.

MARTIN HABERMAN
TOBIE MEISEL

*Dance—An Art in Academe*

# Introduction

## by Bonnie Bird

In view of the tremendous changes occurring in our world today — the planned developments and unpredicted upheavals—it is necessary to reassess where we have been in the field of dance and where we would like to be. In considering one of the least understood arts—the dance—we might start with the question, "What function should dance have in the world of tomorrow?" At present, dance is squashed into a remote corner, much neglected by the main stream and power centers of this country.

During the last seventy-five years, the United States has emerged as the most powerful nation in the world, with the greatest war machine ever developed in history and with the greatest capacity for industrial production, transportation, and distribution. We are daily confronted with the formation of new, complex, diversified corporations; with the invention of new, miraculous materials; with the proliferation of new products to buy, new methods of construction, new ways to make money, new problems for balancing trade, new ways to utilize arts, science, education, entertainment, and news media as adjuncts to the task of distributing goods and forming opinions. In this process, not only the arts but also people have been left in a secondary place, insignificant to the dynamic push of the economic life of the country.

We are all now well aware of the counterrevolutions that have sprung up, almost spontaneously, in many parts of the globe. It is not surprising that the "have nots," the dispossessed, and the ghetto dwellers, confronted with great unfulfilled promises and inviting advertisements, have "blown their tops" in

1

reckless frustration. But there have also been various middle-class rebellions. Stemming from the deep underlying need of people to be whole and individual, these movements have special significance. One movement has been toward psychedelic drugs and a non-participatory life on the fringes of society. This trend is noteworthy because it denies the middle-class orientation to success and the conventional social values. Seeking "mind expanders" to bring about new sensory, mystic experiences and insights, dwelling on inner feelings of self-discovering, and seeking more intuitive, non-scientific, non-rational values—all this is reality in our society.

Also characteristic of this revolt is the physical activity of occupying a place, as witness the sit-ins and demonstrations. The physical involvement of university students is a personal effort to protest their disenfranchisement, their feeling of impotence in shaping their education and preparation for a life of their own choosing. In response, their elders seem to them only to offer the draft, and contracts with the major recruiting corporations. There is almost a reveling, simply for sheer self-assertion, for a feeling of power and involvement, in confrontation with university officials and police. The difficulty is that these reactions are as mindless and distorted as the highly structured systems they reject are impersonal and automated. Too many of the activities of these alienated groups seem to have no significant goals, no thought-out frames of reference; they are random, shapeless, spontaneous, emotional outbursts. They stand in sharp contrast to the planned, reasoned, disciplined program and tactics worked out by Rev. Martin Luther King, Jr., and his Southern Christian Leadership Council.

What is lacking in our lopsided society is the humanizing counterbalance of the arts: the spirit of fantasy, of imagination, of lives concerned with values, with depth of feelings and understanding, of inventive creativity. It takes an economic base to support such a culture. The ancient Greeks lived off a slave-operated economy; but we can do better in our industrialized economy, if only we can agree to manage these resources toward more human ends. Our ordinary citizens are not really the robots Chaplin satirized in "Modern Times"; neither is our man in the street "The Man in the Gray Flannel Suit" or "The Ugly American."

Dance is one of the neglected arts that our society needs badly. One can gain perspective regarding the relationship of dance to humanness by considering (1) the primary elements of dance as they are involved in the development of the child, and (2) dance as a social activity changing its style and functions from primitive to contemporary times.

From the earliest moments of life, man lives in his body—he is from birth to death continuously in action. The range and variety of his motion are enormous. His body is the unique instrument for living his life. It is more than that; it is the center of his experience, for it is not only fundamental to his perception and conceptualization but reflects what has been perceived and conceptualized.

For months the newborn babe can do very little; he has no eye-hand coordination, no locomotion; he uses no tools. But he can feel, and his feeling is expressed through movement. Observing adults can recognize elation, eagerness, surprise, wonder, fury, and much more. With our emphasis upon verbal learning, many of us tend to forget that however advantageous words are for communicating, movements and gestures, facial expressions and voice inflections also carry a great load of meaning, often completely negating verbal content. A typescript of a conversation is pretty pale in comparison with the live action.

There are many occasions when movement is, in fact, the message: the "pained" expression, the raised eyebrow, the scowl of intimidation, the footwork or finger-tapping of impatience, the disarming smile—these are potent items in the currency of social interchange, though hardly acknowledged consciously. Non-verbal communication is the basic skill of clowns, actors in the silent movies, and the great mimes.

Many body movements are preparatory, like "getting set," and are not intended as signals to others; but they may be "read" by sensitive people and the action anticipated. The poker player puts on his poker face to try to circumvent such "reading." Football and basketball players try to get clues from the opponents' moves in order to anticipate them. Despite one's desire not to reveal himself, one's expression, posture, and tensions are unconsciously revealing.

The act of being born might well be considered the very first step in the long process of discovering oneself. Then, within a matter of days, the infant is involved in establishing an acquaintance with his arms, legs, mouth, head and the sensory fields; gaining command of his arms, hands, fingers, tongue, voice, head; gradually perceiving his contours; separating himself from the rest of the environment; becoming aware of the relationship between himself and whatever his mother may seem to mean to him.

From the age of four, movement provides an important basis for one's sense of self—for one's self-image. It provides the groundwork for awareness of the body—its inner sense of moving is the basis for the autonomy of the individual and for the distinction of boundaries between self and non-self, me and not-me.

Since it is vital to the healthy growth of the human being to move freely, it is the right of every child to be provided with opportunities to participate in a wide range of expressive movement experience throughout his school years. It may be that the range of relationships in the child's world are narrow, constricted, stereotyped, as now seen in urban and rural poverty areas. Imaginative dance experiences can counter these forces by offering expanded emotional experience amplified by the imagery of creative teaching situations. In such an atmosphere feelings can be better understood by the child, for there the purity of unadulterated imaginative fantasy is acceptable and not corroded by practical hard reality. Rage, fear, love, consideration, wonder, triumph, achievement, pride, confidence—all may be experienced and savored again and again!

For children of all ages and social conditions, the objectives of dance are these:

To lead them in a variety of physical activities which acquaint them consciously with the functions and relationships of the moving parts of their bodies.

To introduce concepts of time-space and energy related to the movement of their bodies, alone and with others.

To encourage them to take pride in achieving control and skill in moving in particular (dramatic, expressive) ways.

To provide situations in which they can stretch their imaginations by "dancing out" (acting out through dance) how their friends, neighbors, relatives, or people in other cultures and times might have felt and behaved.

To encourage individual creativity in exploration and discussion of ideas, at the same time reinforcing the values of self-control and appreciation for others' ideas and accomplishments. By dancing out certain crucial and significant situations, feelings may be better understood and brought under control; and self-control may be extended to the balanced control of nature.

A program based on such objectives results in greater confidence as the individual becomes self-actualized, motivated from within, a more mature, whole individual.


Let us turn now to dance as an art. We may ask: In what ways is dance an art, similar to but different from painting, music, sculpture, theater? And we might also ask what is included in the art of dance: Does it include ballet, modern dance, "self-expression"? Folk dancing, ballroom dancing? Tap? Figure skating, gymnastics?

In most primitive tribes, dance was a most encompassing activity, in that it included dancing, music, percussion, dramatization, vocalization, masks and decoration, make-up and costumes, all in one. Most important, dancing was a central part of living: as an integrative force it served to teach the traditions and roles; it was the way of exercising religious rituals; through dance and incantations, efforts were made to communicate with and to control heavens and earth, other men and nature, crops and game, life and death. Living and dancing were one. Children were brought up dancing.

With the development of more complex and elaborate civilizations, with written languages and with class distinctions as found in the Middle Ages and later in Western Europe, many changes occurred. There was opportunity for a specialization and separation of aspects of the arts. With the rise of wealthy patrons—whether merchants, prelates, or princes—the spectacular dance, separating the skilled performers from a passive audience, arose. The church could install organs, choirs, and solo performers; royalty could have its command performances, could induce dancers to invent new forms and styles of dancing and romantic stories appropriate to the special tastes of the court. As populations and urban centers grew, as royalty gave way to republicanism, and as the arts began to develop specialist groups, histories, and traditions of their own, there evolved a separation of audiences for the arts. Ballet is sustained largely in its older romantic traditions, for the elite audiences; and critics have been employed to interpret the meaning and evaluate the skills of the performances to the middle class. Folk dancing is now more like a lively or animated collection of antiques, representative of former cultures, a physical activity now removed from its original purposes. Popular dancing develops out of the energy and inventiveness of spirited young people, offering a means of expression and social-sexual relationship. The vital force in dance in this century, the attempt to get back to the roots of expressive feeling in the idiom of the culture, started with Isadora Duncan and flowered with her disciples and their artistic heirs in later generations.

In this country in the twenties, Isadora's dream was caught by young dancers rising from the ranks of the Denishawn Company (Martha Graham, Doris Humphrey, and Charles Weidman), from the Mary Wigman Company (Hanya Holm), even from the Metropolitan Opera Ballet (Helen Tamiris). Vital and insightful young people they were, deeply committed to searching out new forms and a movement language that would express their vision as artists nurtured in a rough-hewn, sprawling new land. Those who have followed— Anna Sokolow, José Limón, Alwin Nikolais, Merce Cunningham, and Jerome Robbins, to name but a few—continue by their work as teachers, performers, and choreographers to enrich and strengthen the extension of dance into the fabric of our national life. Their work challenges us—sets us in motion—in the studios, in the schools, in our theater seats, whenever we come in contact with it. It demands our attention even when non-communication seems to be the communication. It is not a dance satisfied to bathe us in comforting blankets of sensuous cream, leaving us soothed but dulled.

Perhaps it is because of its central concern with the individual as a uniquely expressive person rather than as a potential virtuoso vehicle that this new dance—most often called modern dance—was recognized by perceptive educators as it emerged as being capable of providing students young and old with a primary integrative experience.

Dance in higher education has made steady strides in the intervening years. Nurtured for the most part within departments of physical education (and nearly always offered for women only), it is now moving into its proper place as a full department within the college of fine arts in an increasing number of colleges and universities.

Hopeful and good as all this is, it is not enough. What of the millions of children in our elementary and secondary schools who have never seen live dancers or consciously experienced the joy of dancing through space? To move is their biological inheritance; to dance is their natural right. The potential rewards are incalculable; for when the child is attended, guided, and encouraged, he unfolds and he creates. His products satisfy him and enrich his world. Dance has a vital contribution to make to society. It is in the interest of defining the "what" and the "how" of such a contribution that the succeeding chapters in this volume are presented.

# I

# Dance as Art

Even the dance purist recognizes that dance exists within a framework partly constructed of the other arts. It draws from their resources and is enhanced by this interrelationship. But even more importantly, the uniqueness of dance cannot be fully appreciated unless the basic elements of the related arts are explored, revealing commonalities and divergencies. Dr. Phenix's chapter elucidates the complementary and distinctive qualities in the interrelationship of dance and the other arts. Dr. Dimondstein discusses conceptual and perceptual elements of the arts, utilizing a space-time-force construct.

# 1

# Relationships of Dance to Other Art Forms

## by Philip H. Phenix

It is worth while to reflect on the relationships of dance to other art forms, as well as to non-aesthetic experiences, in order to understand better the distinctive significance of dance and the particular contribution it may make to the enrichment of human life. Such reflection may also yield insights concerning the ways in which the various art forms may mutually complement one another.

Relationships among the arts may be conceived in several different senses. First, there are auxiliary relationships, signifying the direct utility that one art has for another. In the case of the dance, the classic auxiliary relationship is to music, in that dances have commonly been accompanied by music, and many musical forms have found their inspiration in the dance. Again, dance may be auxiliary to drama, through providing expressive forms to enhance the actor's movements. A dance is also frequently regarded essentially as an alternative way of telling a story that has been related in a novel, play, or poem. Sculpture, architecture, painting, and design also are clearly important auxiliaries to the art of dance, through providing appropriate stage settings and costumes for the dancers.

Auxiliary relationships introduce the problem of aesthetic integrity, which arises whenever art forms are mixed. Each art form has a distinctive modality which tends to be confused and compromised by mixed productions. What purports to be a help may thus become a hindrance to effective aesthetic expression. For this reason, it became important in modern times to liberate dance from any necessary connection with music. Similarly, a dance that simply purports to tell a story degenerates into pantomime. The meaning of a dance is not exhausted in relating a story; and to hold that it is, is to accept the same aesthetic impoverishment that occurs when program notes are taken as a verbal equivalent of a musical composition. In like manner, too much focus on the pictorial impressions of scenery and costume designs may deflect the spectators from primary attention to the dance movements.

Aesthetic integrity requires that auxiliary relationships really help—that the auxiliary arts be subordinated to the aesthetic intention of the dance, so as to contribute to the fulfillment of its distinctive aesthetic possibilities.

A second sense of relationships concerns the formal properties that dance shares with other arts. Here one asks not how other arts enter substantively into the dance, but how the nature of dance may be understood better through a comparative analysis of art forms. Such an analysis may not only deepen understanding but also provide a basis for assessing the desirability of auxiliary relationships.

Dance shares with other art forms the features that distinguish art objects from all other things. A dance provides a sense presentation deliberately created to evoke an aesthetic, as opposed to a utilitarian, response in the observer. Its fundamental office is to create in the percipient a significant emotion, valuable in itself, and not merely to serve as an instrument of some other purpose. Each dance is a unique composition, expressing its own intrinsic being, and as such is subject only to its own inherent norms. On the part of the observer, this general aesthetic qualification entails that each dance work be approached with a radical openness to what it distinctively signifies, with a minimum of critical predisposition about what it ought to mean. Likewise, it follows that the evaluation of a dance should be based on the intrinsic qualities it exhibits and not on extrinsic factors, except as the latter have been assimilated into the aesthetic form itself.

It is on these general aesthetic grounds that the similarities in the modern climate of creation and perception in dance and in the other arts, notably in music, painting, and sculpture, may be understood. Modern music is characterized by a high degree of experimental innovation in formal patterns. In painting and sculpture too, radical departures from classical norms are not only accepted but acclaimed. In music, standard structures of tonality have been transcended so as to admit very intricate sound patterns demanding a high degree of order-perception on the part of the listener. In painting and sculpture, the criterion of form-recognizability, i.e., the demand that the work of art look like something with which one is already familiar, has been abandoned in favor of a principle of free design-creation. These modern tendencies do not exclude the use of classical forms: modern music may still be tonal and visual designs may still be representational; the point is that the standard patterns of the past are not artistically obligatory.

This change in the modern expectation is not, as it is often conceived to be, merely a shift in styles, from "classical" to "modern." It expresses a fundamental revolution in aesthetic outlook, from the conception of a work of art as a substitute or copy of something else to the realization that the artist creates a new world. The essence of artistic creation is the transformation of the existing order of things. Hence the normal aim of the artist is not to reproduce the recognizable but to produce a new perceptible reality. Even when familiar forms are employed, the distinctive artistic achievement consists in their transfiguration so as to generate a fresh mode of perception.

The art of dance shares in this general recasting of aesthetic expectation. Modern interpretive dance manifests the new freedom of expressive form. The more traditional forms of classical ballet have also been influenced by the modern outlook, opening the way to greater range and variety of movement patterns. Nevertheless, in respect to the relation of its art forms to existing reality, the dance occupies a unique position among the arts. This uniqueness stems from the fundamental fact that the human body is the material basis for the dance. In every other art form, with the partial exception of acting and singing, the artist creates the work of art and sets it free to become an independent center of expressive power. The forms of a poem, a painting, a statue, or a sonnet are not directly limited by the formative capabilities of the human body, but embrace a limitless range of non-bodily formal possibilities. Musical sounds and paintings can be extravagant to a degree that dance forms can never be, for the human body keeps the latter within the compass of the intimately comprehensible, by virtue of the body's recognized natural limitations.

On this account, the dance can never transcend a certain fundamental realism. It can never contradict, as can surrealist painting, sculpture, music, or poetry, the basic integrity of the natural reality. Accordingly, dance is saved from the extremes to which some artists go in search of novelty in the name of the aesthetic principle of reality-transfiguration.

But this anchorage of dance in the reality of the body does not limit it to the domain of the prosaic and comfortably familiar. The dancer, like his counterparts in other arts, achieves aesthetic effect through inducing a powerful illusion. The forms the body assumes in dance are qualitatively extraordinary. They disclose potentialities of posture and movement that transcend normal existence. Thus, the dance creates an ideal structure of heightened possibilities, which owes its special aesthetic impact to the viewer's awareness that these are his own potentialities, because they are realized in bodies like his own.

This fact that body movements are the materials from which dance forms are constructed suggests a third possible type of relationship to other art forms —a relationship that is neither auxiliary in the strict sense nor one of formal similarity. All aesthetic response includes kinesthetic elements. Aesthetic perception is not pure intellection, as scientific cognition is. In the arts, the percipient reacts with his whole being, integrated of body and mind. Intellect and sense are united in one total response. Poetry moves not only the mind but in its rhythms engages the pulses of the body. Painting evokes not only visual responses but muscular tensions and releases corresponding to the spatial organization of the work. Music, too, evidently achieves its effect through the association of its patterns of rhythm and pitch with the vital periodicities of circulation, respiration, and nervous excitation.

The pivotal role of dance among the arts is due to the fact that the kinesthetic element, which gives sensuous reality to aesthetic perception in all of the arts, is deliberately and systematically cultivated in the art of dance. For this reason dance may be regarded as a preparation or conditioner for participation in all of the other arts. Familiarity with dance ought to enhance perceptivity to the other arts by virtue of the kinesthetic sensitization it affords; and the vitality and dissemination of the art of dance may be preconditions for optimum aesthetic development in all branches of art.

Closely connected with the kinesthetic relationship of dance to the other arts is a historic-genetic relationship which has a bearing on the nature of the formal relationships. Dance is the primordial art. It is the original, undifferentiated form of aesthetic action, in which the person concretizes significant forms by means of his own being, as an organic whole. Music is a specialization of this primordial response, through emphasizing, extending, and refining the temporal periodicities of the dance. Painting and sculpture specialize in the visual patternings presented in the dance. Each art may be analyzed as an elaboration, and usually also as an augmentation, through the use of materials other than the human body, of elements present in the dance. While very specialized, however, art is never severed; and therefore dance art continues as a vivifying potentiality in the whole range of aesthetic specializations.

It remains to mention in more detail some of these salient formal relationships between dance and each of the other major arts. Sculpture has a striking likeness to dance in that both are presentations of three-dimensional spatial configurations. The crucial factor in both is the balancing of masses in a gravitational field in such a way as to elicit emotional tension and resolution through the contemplation of complementary material components. The difference is that most sculptured objects do not move, as dancers do, so the illusion of motion must be created by dynamic tensions inherent in the material arrangement. It should be noted that even non-human forms in sculpture achieve their effect through imaginative subjective transformation into bodily configurations in which the percipient participates.

Architecture, like sculpture, shares with dance the aesthetic effect of palpable masses in gravitational equilibrium. A well-designed building stands gracefully and impressively as a complementary concatenation of material components in balanced tension of masses. The "feel" of its columns and vaults is, as it were, a projection of the corresponding tensions of limbs and torso in the dance. Moreover, since the building is designed to provide living space within, the architect conceives his structural forms in relation to the bodily postures of those who will inhabit it. The space-creating forms of the architect's design may thus be regarded as complementary to the forms of human configuration celebrated and aesthetically exploited in the dance. Hence it can be argued that significant creation and perception in architecture presuppose the kinesthetic imagination that is the defining feature of the art of dance.

Painting is a step further removed in the direction of abstraction from the solid embodiment of dance, sculpture, and architecture. Nevertheless, the perceptual effect of paintings still depends on spatial distribution in a gravitational field. Every painting is an equilibrium of complementary lines and apparent volumes and masses in relation to the vertical axis. Just as the quintessence of aesthetic effect in the art of dance is the progressive dynamic equilibrium that continually saves the dancer from falling in a heap and enables him to wrest victories from the gravitational adventures he deliberately undertakes, so in painting the success of the composition depends on the effective resolution of vital tensions and balancing of contrasts.

Sculpture, architecture, and painting constitute relative abstractions from the wholeness of dance in respect to spatial forms, prescinding from its temporal flow. These three arts of space create the illusion of motion, rather than its sensible reality. Musical art, in contrast, abstracts from the dance its temporal forms. Its essence is the patterning of sounds in temporal sequence, and its aesthetic effect is achieved through memory and anticipation, which are also of basic importance in dance. Moreover, music, though substantially temporal, creates the illusion of space relations by virtue of pitch. It is no accident, but rather a consequence of a basic formal relationship, that notes are described as "high" and "low"—terms of spatial reference. For this reason, musical sounds can be regarded as aesthetic analogues of bodily positions. Musical sequences may be analyzed as corresponding perceptively to rising and falling movements, and choral patterns as complex postures involving one or many dancers. In this way music may be considered formally as a translation of dance movements into rhythmic tonal sequences, and vice versa.

In the case of music a further distinction needs to be made between the arts of composition and of performance. In performance the formal correspondences to the art of dance are reinforced by the actualities of body movement required in singing or playing an instrument. Thus, the kinesthetic ingredients of music are even more extensive and obvious for the performing artist than for the composer. As for the listener, his kinesthetic resonances partake of those both of composer and performer.

The language arts present problems of special interest and difficulty in relation to the art of dance. The use of words opens up to the artist boundless resources of expressive possibility. It would appear that the world thus disclosed would far transcend the relatively limited domain of the dance and hence that the relationships between dance and poetry or drama would be relatively distant. But the more one reflects on the import of language, the more doubtful this conclusion appears. Modern theories of knowledge put great emphasis on the behavioral specification of meanings. Language consists of systems of symbols that create surrogates for actual experiences. It follows that the language arts create aesthetic effects which in the last analysis may be semantically rooted in concrete human action, which is prototypically presented in the dance.

Poetry, like music, in its ostensible form is a time art, depending on rhythmic sequences for its effect. But with words instead of tones, a far wider range of meanings is available, and the relevant behavioral counterparts presentable in dance form are correspondingly more complex. Of all the arts, drama at first appearance most resembles the dance, in that living persons act out the work of art in a composition framed both in space and time. However, in drama the aesthetic effect is not, as in dance, achieved primarily through extraordinary bodily postures, but through the dramatic structure contained in the spoken lines. The deeper relationship of drama to dance consists in the possibility of postural interpretation of the central dramatic meanings. The behavioral interpretations of the dramatic metaphors will, as dance postures, be as profoundly moving as the drama is dramatically significant.


In sum, what emerges from close reflection on the relationship of dance to the other arts is that the various art forms have significant identities that distinguish them from other cultural forms, and that among the arts dance occupies a singularly central position. The auxiliary and formal relationships can be seen on careful analysis to be rooted in a fundamental ontological relationship stemming from the ultimate connection of human meanings to the concrete acts of the complete person. Since dance is the art in which such acts are most purely and simply exhibited for aesthetic contemplation, it is important to the vitality and the intimate appreciation of all the arts that the art of dance be effectively cultivated.

# 2

# Space-Time-Force: An Aesthetic Construct

## by Geraldine Dimondstein

While each art form has its own distinguishing characteristics, its unique image, and its particular media, the realm of the arts exists within a larger world—that of space-time-force, into which enter the common conceptual and perceptual elements. Each component occupies a central position in the way an individual responds to his environment: to perceptual elements which function on the level of sensation and emotion, and to conventional, metrical standards, fixed by physical laws. Both types of response are inherent in all human behavior, but they differ in quality and form according to what is expressed and the mode of expression.

Since the arts deal with the objectification of feelings expressed through symbolic, tangible form, we are concerned with a very special aspect of human behavior. In everyday life, the outcome of any interaction between an individual and his environment is experience. In the arts, the experience is one of participation and communication by means of the senses. Such interaction, however, does not occur in a generalized, amorphous environment, but in a space-time environment which one defines by the way he orders his perceptions and concepts. Force, too, becomes a component, in the very manner in which energy or tension is projected in an art form. Its effects can be observed in the way an individual establishes his own dimensions of space and time.

If we analyze the space-time-force construct, we begin to see the difference between the conceptual and the perceptual, or between the "real" world and the "feeling" world. We can also observe how this construct is expressed in relation to dance, sculpture, and painting.

## SPACE

On a conceptual level, space becomes known to us as it exists in the physical world, through shapes, sizes, and relationships. It involves ideas about our bodies in space, objects in space, and the spatial relationships within the environment to which we orient ourselves. Spatial perception begins with the body as the center of reference which determines the way we use space. As one becomes increasingly aware of his body, he also becomes aware of the dimensions of other objects and people in the environment. But the use of space to create an aesthetic form is not rational or logical—it is expressionist and sensuous. One's own perception of space becomes a source which determines how he sets limits or expands space in any creative effort.

Dance has been described as a "space art," a "time art," and a "form in space-time." Such definitions do not adequately describe the total experience in which dance movement exists. Dance is distinguished from the other arts in that all of the elements of space-time-force are essential in forming the dynamic image. The body moves through space, in time, and in relation to gravity. Movement is conceived, executed, and understood only through the interrelationship of these elements. As aesthetic qualities, they take the form of created rather than conventional gestures, and become the connective tissue from which a personal movement vocabulary is developed.

Space as an abstract, physical entity is meaningless unless it serves as a vehicle for emotional expression. It must be occupied, contained, defined. A dancer defines space by his very presence. The area in which he exists becomes occupied, just as by the sculptured object. Even when immobile, he defines space; we can see around him, follow the plastic lines of his body, and know that he has dimension. Beyond this, the space between the individual and the walls, or between himself and other people or objects, is also defined. Technically, space in dance is defined in terms of direction, range, level. Qualitatively, however, it is expressed only in relation to an individual's needs to project ideas and emotions through the unique use of his body.

In painting and sculpture, the difference in the use of space is a more basic consideration than whether we are dealing with a two- or three-dimensional image. Sculpture is concerned with the creation of volumes that displace or inhabit space. The creative process involves shaping material into physical forms to occupy a particular space, as well as the space immediately surrounding it. It is the complement of empty space around the sculpture that produces a tension or movement between what is occupied in it and what is not, and the external space becomes part of the sculptural volume.

Sculpture may be regarded as a visual-kinetic image, to clarify certain misconceptions—that the use of space in painting and sculpture is the same, and that merely different means are used to achieve the same ends. A painting is involved with projecting only one real relationship to the observer. As a composition, it presents a single face which exists in a created space. A sculpture is not concerned with one static system of relationships, but is a volume which exists in actual space.

In sculpture, a unified form is created out of elements which are also elements of painting—movement, rhythm, line, texture. But it is the multiple qualities of their relationships which produce the characteristics unique to sculpture as a three-dimensional image. Painting is a projection of space onto a flat surface; a sculpture, by its very nature, is a thing in itself. In the sculptural process, every silhouette is expressed three-dimensionally and projects a different form. The notion of sculpture as an object which displaces actual space leads to an awareness that all points of view are important, and that all are integral to the whole.

Thus, while sculpture and painting both involve the use of created space, painting draws from visual sensory data and shapes space which is viewed frontally and directly. Sculpture, on the other hand, produces a volume which is originally created through the sense of touch, and is therefore both a visual and a tactual experience. Langer's concept that the problem of sculpture is "making tactual space visible" illuminates the essence of the process.[1]

Painting is most generally described as a "space art," but such definition may equally apply to dance or sculpture. It is only in pursuing its pictorial qualities that we learn how to see it, for visual art, as differing from the tactile and kinesthetic, is made primarily for sight.

Space exists all around us in the real world; it is the very stuff of our environment. Yet, we must learn to orient ourselves to space in particular ways. As children, we begin to identify spatial relationships by hearing, moving, seeing, touching. Such sensing becomes an unconscious part of our daily behavior as we deal with actual spatial phenomena. In creating a painting, however, space is not experiential. Although painting draws from memory images of sight and touch, sound and motion, it is an entirely visual space which is organized.

Ultimately, pictorial space is created and resides only within the realm of some boundary or frame. A painting is not an actual space but is analogous to the space in which we live. Sculpture, on the other hand, exists in continuity with external space and has a life beyond the boundaries of its contours. Dance, through movement, has not only a spatial existence (like a painting) and a tactual quality (like a piece of sculpture), but the added dynamic element of *change* in space.

## TIME

A space-time-force construct has objective and subjective dimensions which are applicable to an analysis of time as well as space. In objective terms, time is composed of calendar and clock intervals which are formally arranged in a before-and-after sequence. Perceived as experience, time is directly related to the rhythms of the body and its world. Just as the space of experience is not the

[1] Susanne K. Langer, *Feeling and Form* (New York: Charles Scribner's Sons, 1953), p. 90.

space of geometry, perceived time is not established by clocks. A unit of time in creative movement may be long or short, great or small, past or present, according to the quality of feeling expressed. In any case, it represents a temporal order self-imposed by an individual. Subjective time is neither pragmatic nor conventionally defined. It is a perceptual element which exists entirely within a given, presented experience.

In dance, just as space cannot be grasped unless limited, so time must be partitioned and made relative to be understood. Time is expressed through the rhythm of the human body as pulse, heartbeat, breath. That an individual reflects his inherent rhythmic functions (has a unique time sense) in movement may be realized by observing him walk across the floor without accompaniment. In all likelihood, the beat which he establishes will have a relationship to his own heartbeat or energy organization. Thus, the essence of one's response to rhythm is both a kinesthetic awareness of his own underlying pulse, and a phenomenon in force-time.

Since the use of time as an aesthetic element is subjective, an individual creates his own rhythmic patterns which may or may not conform to metrical or musical standards. A young child, given the freedom, may respond not to the rhythm he hears, or to the one offered by the teacher, but to the rhythm he feels. An individual's own movement inventions have a rhythmic structure, and once aware of them he can develop them into a movement vocabulary.

The existence of time as a significant element in painting and sculpture is a philosophical issue. Whether time functions in forming the sculptural image is still debated among philosophers and aestheticians. If it does, it exists in the variation of contours and profiles seen in the round, and in the time it takes for one to perceive the object in all of its spatial roundness. Painting and sculpture utilize two of the dimensions of external reality, space and force; but both arts inherently lack time. Pictures do not begin at one moment and end at another. While the pictorial image is created over time, in space-force, the painting itself is physically static and does not change. With sculpture, too, time exists as experience which assumes a period of contemplation. In either case, time is not sequential; it is immediate in its presence.

## FORCE

Concepts of force involve ideas of weight, gravity, energies in motion, and relationships in space. A perception of force is expressed as tension or stress, experienced as energy. In painting it is revealed through line, color, or shape; in sculpture, by the tensions in the volumes or contours; in dance, by the flow and control of energy. In all art forms, force is revealed as dynamics which are inherent in any space-time relationship. One imbues this element with his own energies and tensions, and embodies it within the total, sensuous form.

In creative movement or dance, force deals with greater or lesser tension, with resistance or acquiescence to the pull of gravity, with heaviness or light-ness. By varying the amount of energy expended and by realeasing energy in alternate ways, different qualities of movement are achieved. Force involves the release or control of energy expressed through the dynamics of contrast and change—fast-slow, up-down, loud-soft. We perceive these qualities with a kinesthetic awareness of movement tension within our own bodies. In order to increase this awareness of tension and sense its aesthetic value, we must "feel" it, as well as intellectually "know" it.

There are innumerable ways in which we can experience an awareness of tension. Most basic, perhaps, are those which involve a consciousness of one's own sense of gravity, and the feeling which comes with the transference of body weight. It is not possible to identify a specific center of gravity for the human body in general, since each individual's body is unique. It is possible, however, through exploration with movement, to eventually locate one's own center. For example, one can sense that as soon as he moves from an aligned position, either by moving any part of his body or in taking a step, there is a change in body weight. It soon becomes apparent that body weight and bal-ance are closely related. One can sense this relationship as it functions in different space-time patterns, expressed by changes in dynamics.

Through continuous explorations with space-time-force, one comes to real-ize that hands, feet, arms, head are capable of moving at different speeds and with different intensity; that the torso can show both heavy and light move-ments, in varying amounts of space and time; and that the whole body moves as an integrating and expressive medium.

Sculpture, as a spatial-kinetic image, derives its force from its internal qual-ities of plasticity and movement. Plasticity is a quality of something that can be molded or shaped; and it characterizes a form that is developing, forming, growing. Force also derives from the tension of contours in relation to both internal and external space. In sculpture as in dance, movement is not ab-stracted from the form itself (as in the projected limbs of a figure or in some type of gesture), but has an integral, expressive function. The force of dance movement is extended in space and time, while sculpture receives its vitality from the flow and intensity of its volumes.

All of the elements of painting—line, color, texture—function as dynamic components which, in juxtaposition, produce tension or opposition on the pic-ture plane. These qualities, in aesthetic relationships, constitute the force in painting. One may not always consciously set about to create a state of equil-ibrium or tension. The sensing of these qualities is in the "doing," and only after a piece of art work is completed do they become objectively observable.

When the movement of forms is met by a countermovement, there is an opposition of energies. We see this in the opposition in direction of single lines; in lines used to define contours that are similar to one another but move in opposite directions (up-down, forward-back); and in shapes or colors that set up a tension which moves spatially within the picture plane (textured against flat forms, contrast between warm and cool colors). Force also emerges from the tension of portraying three-dimensional forms against a two-dimensional surface. Finally, the greatest source of tension, for both creator and beholder, lies in the relationship between that which exists in nature, as the thing perceived, and the transformation of it into a pictorial image.

In sum, then, the aesthetic elements of space-time-force function in the service of perception. We cannot regard them as tools or techniques any more than we can look upon the arts as skills. To analyze gestures in movement, shapes in sculpture, or lines in painting in terms of objective or "scientific" criteria is neither an indication that we understand them inwardly nor a guarantee that we have learned to respond to them with any degree of aesthetic sensibility.

Creative response is highly idiomatic. The use of space in painting or sculpture by one individual may not be applicable by another, and the expression of time and force may vary in movement exploration. These elements, by their very abstract, subjective nature, take different forms in different people. What they do is reflect a relative sense of aesthetic order in each person's perceptual frame of reference.

The aesthetic value of the space-time-force construct is in the individual's ability to define and control the form with which he is involved in such a way that he heightens its emotional impact. Eventually, space-time-force becomes the continuum of integrative elements of perception through which one conceives of forms in ways new for him; that is, we can look for new relationships—new space, new time, new force—for fresh and broadening stimuli.

What we are seeking, even with children, is an awareness in space-time-force of the qualities of experience and expression. To make the transition from experiential factors in daily living to aesthetic elements in the arts requires the very materials and energies of nature. What is created and presented in the arts is therefore not random emotional expression, but organized aesthetic effort.

# II

# Dance and Communication

Dance is a means of natural aesthetic expression. It is reflective of a society and instrumental in shaping it. Dance is an aesthetic point of entry into the analysis of a society's past, present, and future. The study of dance in a historical and sociological context deepens understanding of the realities and aspirations of a people.

But equally important is a converse order: studying the context and situation as a means of understanding the dance. With the first approach one might, for example, examine the popular dances of today in order to infer the values of youth. With the second, one might begin with a study of the Eskimos and their culture, for example, in order to gain fuller understanding and appreciation of certain kinds of dance.

Harriet Berg considers the relevance of dance in today's society, including the role which dance can play for today's young men. Irmgard Bartenieff and Forrestine Paulay discuss results and implications of the Choreometrics Project, in which dance emerges as "a central and vital force" in all societies. They have identified important communicative, cultural elements of dance and work behavior and make recommendations—to the scientist, the educator, and the professional dancer—for acting upon this knowledge. Judith Hanna discusses dance as a cultural expression and as a behavioral process which may be subjected to the methodology of the social sciences and enhanced by their contributions.

# 3

# Dance as Cultural Expression

## by Irmgard Bartenieff and Forrestine Paulay

The special communicative role of the dance, the eldest of the arts, needs now to be reconsidered in relation to the rapid development of the whole field of communication. Where our ancestors lived in a relatively quiet and uneventful world, we moderns are deafened by the roar of gigantic communication systems. A communication business, with media competing for our attention through all the senses, takes up more and more time and space and fattens on our forced responses, while the arts and the goals of true communication suffer. Now that none of us ever need be alone, we are beset by a growing sense of isolation and despair. Indeed there seems to be a correlation between the number of communication devices in the home and the number of books and articles on the alienation of the individual in our society.

The recent history of dance began with a revolt against formalism, against aestheticism, against the view of dance as entertainment and distraction. Our revolutionaries transformed the dance into an expressionistic art form that communicated the reactions of individual souls to the conflicts and problems of the modern world. These impassioned artists shaped the dance and the dance education of today, and even though their work has until very recently been considered highbrow and avant-garde, it has been a strong influence for years on the other arts, notably music and the theater, as well as on education. The "expressive" focus of modern dance has fostered the awareness that children are naturally expressive and that their affinity for the arts may be stimulated at a very early age.

The emphasis on the creative potential of children, and indeed of all individuals, comes as a natural reaction to the accelerating development of technology and the penetration of machines and of big government into every aspect of life. Research, discussion, and experimentation in the arts is going on everywhere. There seems to be a growing recognition of the vital role the arts can play in child development, somehow helping to transform the magic

23

visions of childhood into the ripened creative action of the adult. There has been less consensus, however, on how this desirable goal may be attained. Indeed, for twenty years or more controversy has raged around the issues of technique versus free expression, imitation versus improvisation, structure versus free form, the unifying character of group activity versus the highly self-expressive individual. The pages that follow attempt to put these issues into a fresh perspective, gained in a recent comparative study of ethnic dance.

In the winter of 1965, Alan Lomax at Columbia University invited the writers of this chapter to engage with him in a survey of dance and movement styles as they relate to cultural traditions. Our data were to be from documentary films about many of the world's peoples. Our working hypothesis was one most artists and teachers share, at least unconsciously—that there are communication universals in the dance which everyone reacts to and whose relative presence or absence defines the dance in relation to the culture in which it is found. Our goal was first to find a way of recording these similarities and differences systematically and then to discover whether dance style varied with culture pattern and, if so, what aspects of culture seem to regulate this relationship. Our study encompassed the analysis of 300 films from 150 different human communities on all six continents.

Perhaps the strongest impressions to come out of our two years' immersion in the dances of many peoples are these: (1) The underlying unity and aesthetic integrity of each of the dance patterns we have encountered bears witness to the universal creativity of human beings, no matter how primitive their technology. (2) Dance is a central and vital force in showing and shaping the life style in all societies.

These impressions have changed our point of view as dance educators, because they have stimulated us to rephrase the issue of the individual versus the collective. One main function of dance, no matter how radical its aims, is to reinforce the principal continuities of the culture from which it comes. Thus the expressive role of the individual dance creator is to discover the neglected potentials in or needs of his culture (or some segment of it). This novel perspective on his own culture is what he discovers in himself. Indeed, viewed from a world perspective, the dances of various periods and the dancing styles of different individuals seem to vary only in the sensitivity with which they reflect culture rather than in their absolute novelty or uniqueness. All must conform to the grand style pattern of the culture heritage.

The context of our work on dance was a general study of style in relation to culture, directed by Alan Lomax and Conrad Arensberg in the Department of Anthropology at Columbia and financed by the National Institute of Mental Health. The over-all aim of the project was to discover how the vast collections of recorded primitive and folk song and dance could aid social scientists in understanding the social process. Four years had been spent in a comparative study of song styles, analyzed directly from field recordings by means of a rating system called Cantometrics, a coined word meaning measure of song.

Cantometrics supplies the listener with a series of simple scales on which he can record his impressions of the presence or absence of various qualities in a song performance: tempo, degree of nasality, average length of phrase, level of loudness, degree of choral concert, degree of repetition in the text, and so forth.

The Cantometric coding system standardizes a set of such perceptual scales and enables the analyst to set down the main characteristics of a song performance in a matter of a few minutes. Thus, within two years a team of coders could make an objective and systematic analysis of several thousand song tapes from a balanced sample of the world's cultures—more than two hundred different societies whose social patterns had also been studied and codified. A computer made it possible to manipulate and compose this long body of comparative data about human behavior, to assemble average song performance and cultural profiles for cultures, culture areas, or regions. It produced patterns of constant relationship between song traits and culture traits.

The Cantometric study was the first to prove that an art style is, at least in some very important respects, socially and culturally determined.[1] In very broad terms Lomax and Grauer, co-inventors of Cantometrics, have demonstrated statistically that song style varies by culture region and area and that the historic distributions of the families of man may now be traced purely in terms of song style. The antiquity of some of these song-style distributions indicates that aesthetic pattern may be the most durable of mankind's creations. Moreover, it has been found that many of the important elements of performance style are determined by specific traits of social organization: productive system, level of social complexity, degree of stratification, centralization of political control, male-female interaction pattern, sexual pattern, and others. Thus, as Lomax points out, the symbolic function of song turns out to be a representation and reinforcement of important behavioral patterns in culture.

The kind of descriptive analysis chosen for musical performance style was then undertaken in the vastly more complex job of analyzing dance. The project, called Choreometrics, added another order of validation to the total study. It proceeded on the hypothesis that a culture's dance style was a fore-

---

[1] For detailed presentation of this proposition, together with exhaustive statistical tests, see Alan Lomax, *Folk Song Style and Culture* (Washington, D.C.: American Association for the Advancement of Science, 1968).

shortened representation of its everyday movement style—a reinforcement of those qualities of movement found in survival activities such as work. Thus Choreometrics set out from the beginning on a course more ambitious than that of the preceding study of song—the new project was to describe and compare the typical movement styles of cultures, culture areas, and culture regions, as found in both everyday activity (work) and expressive activity (dance).

We, Bartenieff and Paulay, brought to this operation a set of concepts from the Laban "effort-shape" system, ripened by years of application in dance and in therapy. The effort-shape system diagrams the way movement utilizes space and energy. Our first attempt was to describe, then classify, a set of filmed behaviors from various cultures with the effort-shape system; but we found that the detail we recorded was obscuring the most striking and easily observable contrasts between different movement styles. We began to see that the effort-shape notation system, as Laban designed it, was an efficient tool for describing the differences between individuals within a culture, but not for diagramming intercultural differences.

Two years of experimentation and adaptation have finally produced a satisfactory system for rating movement, based on Laban's concepts but corresponding in level and design to the system of style analysis developed on the Cantometrics project. It has been tested on films from more than 150 cultures and has performed a number of efficient classification operations. When its profiles of movement style are subjected to comparison by the computer, the following results emerge:

1. Work and dance profiles have been shown to have a high degree of similarity within each culture. We are dancing a survival pattern.
2. The profiles of dance cluster together to form style regions which match those discovered by Cantometrics and which correspond to the historic divisions of the families of mankind.
3. Many characteristics, crucial to dance style, have proved to be, as in the case of song style, functions of social and productive complexity.
4. Thus it appears that dance varies by culture type and social structure, as does song.
5. The principal function so far discovered for the dance communication is that it crystallizes and reinforces the set of postural and dynamic traits that identifies their user as a member of a certain culture within one of the grand cultural traditions, such as the Amerindian, the Polynesian, the African. We believe that these culturally transmitted and learned bodily signatures form the base lines for all other behavior, whether communicative, creative, or everyday.

These first discoveries are the joint product of Lomax, Bartenieff, and Paulay. All have been very strongly confirmed by statistical tests upon a sample of 137 cultures for which we have both dance and cultural ratings. The descriptive coding system, now a hundred lines long, is still being tested. It includes observations of the following: body parts habitually involved, body attitude (active stance), shape and dimension of movements, the way direction is changed in movement, movement qualities such as relative smoothness and tempo, torso-limb relationship, kind of synchrony between movers, and features of group formation.

Two of the rating parameters vary cross-regionally and in relation to productive complexity. Examination of the first, body attitude, shows that the basic stance from which all activity is developed is related to culture region, thus becoming a cultural identifier. The second, transition, indicates that simple producers such as hunters and early gardeners carry out their tasks using linear paths and simple, abrupt transitions; the more complex producers, such as advanced agriculturalists, employ a three-dimensional approach to space both in movement path and in transition. It is most important to remember that all these movement traits occur to some extent in all cultures; they are part of a universal vocabulary. Our finding is that they vary in frequency among different types of culture. Thus when we say that simple producers restrict most of their operations to a simple retracing of the same path over and over, this is because both their tools and their tasks demand no more. The elaborate figure-of-eight "loop," most frequent in the rice cultures of Asia, allows for a great freedom of choice in shaping or connecting different spatial phases of an activity; it is employed in planting of the delicate rice shoots and in complex handicrafts such as weaving and carving as well as in the sinuous movement of the dance drama.

Rudolph Laban had early seen that there was a relation between transition and body attitude and culture. He noted that in certain epochs and parts of the world, in particular occupations, in cherished aesthetic creeds or in utilitarian skills, certain attitudes of the body are preferred and more frequently used than others. It is easy to understand how the selection of and preference for certain bodily attitudes create style: yet we must remember it is in the transition between positions that an appropriate change of expression is made, thus creating dynamically coherent movement style.


Choreometrics now enables us to pick out and compare the distinctive cluster of movement qualities for each culture, as Laban suggested. Inspection of Eskimo and Iroquois profiles indicates that the movement profiles for Eskimo and Iroquois dances are very much alike. Indeed, their over-all statistical similarity is 87 points out of a possible 100. As a matter of fact, these two cultures belong to the same cultural and song-style regions. Now their general similarity in dance emerges, in our codings for dynamic qualities, even though we know that the formations and the steps employed by the two cultures are considerably different. Choreometrics, however, can discover and specify the underlying pattern which animates both their expressive and their practical activities and which designates these two cultures as Amerindian. Such findings will be of interest not only to the anthropologist and the folklorist, the artist and the educator, but to the American Indian tribes themselves, as they assume more and more the control over their own cultural destinies.

The Caribou Eskimo confronts his cold environment from the vantage of a wide frontal body stance. His compactly held torso provides a firm base for his incredibly swift blow and straight thrusting actions. Whether he is seen delivering a single blow which kills a seal or, in a more relaxed fashion, striking the edge of a drum head with the drum stick, a simultaneous mode of movement behavior prevails: all body parts moving in unison, in a movement style that yields maximum force. Along with this condensed body functioning goes an economy in the use of space, linear paths predominating, either strictly reversing direction or abruptly changing course with sharp, angular transitions.

Like that of the Eskimo, the stance of the Ellice Island male dancer is also wide; however, it is dissimilar in other important respects. The rhythmic up-and-down motion of the pelvis on widely spread legs establishes a pulsating base for the more intricate use of forearms and hands. The movement style is characterized by slight rocking motions of the chest, and waves of movement rise from the center of the torso and flow segment by segment into forward outstretched arms. This torso style is seen in canoe building as a more gradual inclusion of body parts, and it contributes to the appearance of a smooth flowing use of energy with curving and looping spatial patterns. Straight-line reversals of actions are notably absent.

Thus, in the paired profiles of work and dance from the Eskimo and the Micronesian—from the arctic and the tropics—we have two contrastive style sets, each suitable and functional in its own environment. The Micronesian shows various features associated with productive complexity which are lacking in the Eskimo. For instance, there is a higher variability in his movement vocabulary. The profiles of black Africa and Eastern Asia reveal that each of these has progressively higher scores in respect to movement variability than does Micronesia. This indicates again that in some respects cultures may be rated, purely in terms of movement qualities, as more or less complex, so far as their relation to production is concerned. Other movement features have nothing to do with complexity, however. Thus, no culture's movement style may be said to be more primitive than another's. Indeed, if such ratings *were* suitable, the profile for Western Europe, which strongly resembles that of the North American Indian, might well be dubbed very primitive. Modern anthropology rules out the old-fashioned idea that those cultures which do not conform to the pattern of European life are primitive. Comparative ethnology discovers, rather, that every type of culture represents a rich and complex adjustment by man to a particular human and natural environment. Each movement style described by Choreometrics seems also to be a specialized technique of adjustment, environmentally adaptive and rich in potential.

Since World War II the power and the energy of cultural nationalism have changed the map of the world. Today in America we are beginning to realize that the "melting pot" idea has not worked, that we are a nation of subcultures each of which demands recognition. As dancers, as movement analysts, we can confirm the view of the anthropologist. We see that different cultural styles of movement and of dance are alive in our classrooms and our discotheques. The fact that these vital differences tend to go unrecognized adds fuel to the unrest that seethes in our American cities.

No intelligent Westerner fails to recognize, for instance, the contribution that Africa, specifically as represented by the underprivileged and exploited American Negro, has made to the popular music and dance of this age. For the last hundred and fifty years, since the introduction of the blackface minstrel show to the theatrical audiences of the West, white Europeans have been responding to and trying to assimilate the newest creations of the American Negro people in song and dance. The stylistic integrity, the life-giving properties, the complexity and the beauty of this great style tradition are admitted, and today we are all trying our best to move like blacks on the dance floor. In spite of all of this, however, the educational and the fine-arts establishments do not really recognize this tradition. Its elements are not taught anywhere. Seldom do they play a part in the educational process, even in predominantly black schools. Only in recent years has there been any attempt to develop a serious theatrical establishment where the Afro-American style continuity is employed in the creation of the fine arts.

Part of the reason for this is that limited research techniques, employed largely by white scholars of the past, have failed to show the extent to which African style models have survived in the Americas. Cantometric results show dramatically that the Afro-American pattern, when viewed from a world perspective, is simply a continuation of the great tradition of West African music. American Negro musicians have learned to employ West European instruments, melodic forms, and harmonic styles, but in their hands these become tools for fulfilling stylistic aims that are rootedly African. Although in Choreometrics we have not begun to match the musical research in sample size, the results we have are just as positive.

There is a remarkable similarity between our codings of a dance filmed in a night club in Harlem, during the 1950's, and of a ritual dance, the Dogon, from the West Sudan, a part of Africa from which came many slaves. A comparison of these two profiles shows multiple rhythms in multiple parts of the body, dramatic in both speed and strength, characterizing both the Harlem and the Dogon movement styles. Their movement originates in the torso and seemingly explodes into a rich variety of patterns and directions contributing to the appearance of heightened intensity and extreme changeability. The Harlem dancer shifts the initiation of movement between chest and pelvis, in a sequence identical to that of the Dogon. A marked twisting at the waist, an important feature in both dances, is also seen in Dogon work. This particular turning of the torso enables the men to extend their reach and create the effect of an increased perimeter of movement.

The aesthetic coherence, the unique possibilities of each of these movement profiles should be of special interest to the dance educators of this country. Yet we discover that many of us have neither the training nor the flexibility to grasp the differences in style and to open channels through which the creative energy can flow. Instead, often without wishing to, we continue to impose the Western European model of behavior on *all* our children, no matter what their background, and to hold this model up for admiration, in our fine arts, as if it were somehow *the* ideal.

The potential value of the Choreometric approach for dance teachers and dance students became apparent to us in an actual teaching situation. We observed the movement patterns of a young Negro dancer as she told us of her difficulties in mastering contemporary modern dance and ballet techniques and in finding meaningful movement expression in her own choreography. As she spoke, we noted how she exaggerated the outstanding European stylistic movement qualities—solidly held torso, taut knees, weight carried high onto the balls of her feet, each phase of her straight channeled gestures carefully structured.

As she began to dance for us it became apparent that she developed her movement out of an elaboration of the "line." We asked her to generate the movement from a pulse instead. This we did as an experiment, since we knew the on-going rhythmic pulse to be a core feature of African movement style. She began bouncing up and down, her knees tightly controlled. Gradually, with our direction, she allowed her whole foot to sense the weight of her body. This became visible in a softening of her whole torso, shoulders sinking downwards, chest coming into a gentle opposition with the pelvis. The bouncing continued, its rhythm reinforced by the two units of her torso. Her knees gave up their mocking tautness. As she focused on her breathing, her head and neck began to move with very slight rocking shifts, as if in affirmation of her new awareness, a seconding voice to the long history of polyrhythm in African dance.

We realized that the African life style which had produced this particular movement pattern could reflect only a part of this young woman's life experience here in America. And so, as she spoke again of her struggles to become a dancer, we asked her to let her movement take over her story. This time her actions were linear and strong, frequently directed from her now active torso. As she continued we could see she retained the essential core of her previous experience—the two-unit torso, a high level of flow—and was allowing the movement to grow out of the rhythms of her feelings. She was no longer directing her energy to maintain a Western European body attitude: no longer trying to impose a foreign "base line." She was allowing the movement to service her aims, her values, to reflect the needs and demands of her whole heritage.

We need to recognize that the dancer can, like the American Negro musician, employ the instruments and forms of West European culture to service his own aims. We believe our American dance scene will realize its full potential, will become an integral, functional part of our culture, only when it recognizes the contributions of all our subcultures.

In this process dance instructors and performing dancers will, in turn, fulfill their role: reinforcing the value and integrity of the cultural traditions of *all* our people.

# 4

# Dance and the Social Sciences: An Escalated Vision[1]

## by Judith Lynne Hanna

Dance, conventionally conceived, is a visually perceived ephemeral plastic art in motion. But from another perspective, dance is human behavior composed of purposefully, rhythmically, and culturally patterned sequences of nonverbal body movement and gesture which elaborate what, for the society involved, are ordinary motor activities. Inspired by selected stimuli from a people's intra-psychic and social environments, dance translates these into meaningful expression through the artistic manipulations of movement. As such expression, dance is shaped by the values, attitudes, and beliefs of the people who comprise its "host" society; it depends on their feeling, thinking, and acting patterns. Thus, the elements of space, rhythm, and dynamics, in their combination and consequent form and style, do not exist apart from the human behavioral processes which produce them. It is for this reason that dance, which *can* be viewed impressionistically, may *also* be subjected to the same objective, systematic observations, analyses, and reporting as are other forms of human behavior.

This is where social and cultural anthropology, sociology, social psychology, economics, political science, and branches of history and human geography enter the picture. The methodologies of these social sciences permit us to go beyond subjective intuition, contemplative perception of the creative product, technical dance descriptions, and the appreciation of dance for its own intrinsic qualities. Social science provides insights into the sources from which dance emanates and the "external" dynamics within which movement can be understood. It enables us to understand the process as well as the product, the relationships of dance to individual personalities, social relationships, political actions, economic transactions, cultural manifestations, historical developments, and geocultural dispersions, as well as the movements themselves.

[1] I wish to thank Professor William John Hanna for his essential contributions to this article.

The social scientist strives for understanding in order to explain, to predict, and even to control (i.e., manipulate man's environment for better living conditions). His methods are far different from the all-too-common impressionistic observation of a social phenomenon. Characteristic of the social scientist's approach to research are the following: public detailed disclosure of methods and results, precise definitions of concepts, objective unbiased data collection, and the development of an organized system of verified propositions ("truths").

The distinctions between art as product and art as process, and between impressionistic and scientific bases of knowledge, are schematically presented below. The primary focus of the social sciences (the shaded area of the diagram) is dance *scientifically* studied as a *process*. Of course, other specialists have different concerns; for example, poets have historically been most interested in the impressionistic observation of dance as a product.

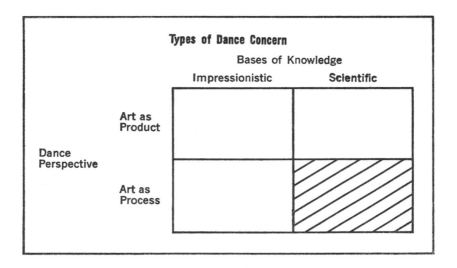

To substantiate the claim that social science can escalate our vision of dance —that art and science are intimately related—I will indicate how the main social sciences might approach the study of dance and how they can contribute to the field of dance.

## CONTRIBUTIONS OF THE SOCIAL SCIENCE DISCIPLINES

The substantive concerns of the various social sciences are so broad that considerable overlap exists. There is, for instance, relatively little difference in this respect between sociology and social anthropology, or between political science and political sociology. To illustrate potential contributions to the field of dance, I shall focus here on what are perhaps core concerns or approaches of each discipline.

*Anthropology,* the "study of man," is seemingly the most comprehensive discipline. However, one school of thought defines the core anthropological interest as "the description and explanation of similarities and differences among human ethnic groups."[2] From this position, the obvious first step in the study of dance is to describe the behavior involved; and for this, collaboration between social scientists and choreologists is usually required. Once the behavior is described, it is possible to identify similarities and differences ranging from the movements performed to the participants involved. A final step in the anthropologist's task is to explain his findings. Why is it, for instance, that the dances of some African ethnic groups are predominantly earthward-oriented with forward inclined torso, tilted pelvis, and bent knees, whereas others tend to maintain an upright posture? A possible explanation may be found in the correlation of the former with an agricultural economy, the latter with pastoralism.

*Sociology* is concerned with patterns of social organization, with relationships among individuals and groups under varying circumstances. In terms of dance, the interest is primarily threefold: relationships among members of a performing group, relationships between dancers and other persons, and relationships between the dance group and others.

Determining leadership structure of a dance group and the factors which are involved in the selection process helps the observer explain choreographic patterns, time and place of performance, dress, and accompaniment. It might be that, in some society, movements are chosen by specified dance leaders, old age is the key criterion of dance leadership, and elderly people are supposed to move sedately. An uninformed observer might conclude that the physical potential of the dance leader determines movement, when in fact the movement is simply an outcome of the process of leadership selection.

Concern about the relationship between dancers and other persons directs attention to such questions as the status of dancers in society. Statuses in a social system are differentiated by the rights and duties attached to them, as well as by their prestige. Historically, dancers have had widely varying statuses; for example, they have been magically endowed bearers of traditions, as well as denigrated prostitutes injecting some art into their exhibitions.

The relationship between the dance group (including the activity of the dance) and others calls attention to the functions of dance in society. Dance

[2] Joseph H. Greenberg, "Anthropology: The Field," in David L. Sils (ed.), *International Encyclopedia of the Social Sciences* (New York: The Macmillan Co. and Free Press, 1968), Vol. 1, p. 305.

might manifestly be an activity purely for personal enjoyment while at the same time performing such latent functions (not recognized by most participants and observers) as socialization—including education. As a quasi-language, dance is sometimes able to communicate as effectively as verbal language itself—and sometimes more so. (Of course, dance communication is universal only with regard to representational forms.) Its audio-visual potential is unique, involving the sight of moving performers in time and space, the sounds of physical movements, the smells of physical exertion, and the feelings of kinesthetic activity or empathy.[3]

*Social psychology* is concerned with the "process whereby the individual learns the beliefs and values of his social group and learns to adjust his behavior so that it meets the expectations of others in the group."[4] The social psychologist, then, might explore dance as a means of establishing personal identity or coping with threatening situations, or as a vehicle of catharsis. For example, initiation dances in some societies mark the transition of an individual from childhood to adulthood, or from commoner to member of a special cult. (An American equivalent is the debutante ball.) Through dance, an individual may achieve mastery of a traumatic situation in a harmless activity which is enjoyable. Among the Ubakala people in Africa, several of the young girls' dances focus upon the anxieties associated with marrying, leaving a familiar home environment to live among strangers, becoming fertile, and bearing children.[5] (The latter is especially dangerous without modern medical treatment; tragedy may occur for seemingly inexplicable reasons.) American popular dance themes focus on similar problems of adolescence—unrequited love, alienation, lonesomeness. With regard to dance as a vehicle of catharsis, a specialist in psychodynamics wrote: "The rhythm, vigorous movements, their coordination and synchronization, tend to induce some degree of catharsis. . . . The essential psychological function of the dance, in fact, is the prevention of depression and accumulation of other psychic stresses."[6]

*Economics,* a discipline concerned with the allocation of scarce resources and the full use of available resources, can also add to our understanding of dance. The performance of a dance involves the allocation of space in which to perform, societal time for performance, payment of performers, material for costumes, and so forth. It should be possible, therefore, to calculate the resources customarily allotted to dance, the additional resources members of a

---

[3] See Judith Lynne Hanna, "African Dance as Education," in *Impulse 1965: Dance and Education Now,* pp. 48-52; and Judith Lynne Hanna & William John Hanna, "Nkwa di Iche Iche: Dance-Plays of Ubakala," *Présence Africaine,* No. 65 (1968), 13-38.

[4] Harold B. Gerard, "Social Psychology," in Sils, *op. cit.,* Vol. 14, p. 460.

[5] Hanna & Hanna, *op. cit., passim.*

[6] Adeoye T. Lambo, "The Place of the Arts in the Emotional Life of the African," *American Society of African Culture Newsletter,* VII, No. 4 (1965), 4.

society will apportion in order to maintain its dance tradition, and the value of dance thus measured (in economic terms) to various societies.

Such a framework serves to emphasize the importance of Fernandez' research on dance as a form of economic exchange among the Pahouin of western Equatorial Africa. He found that if a visiting troupe's performance in a foreign village excites the local people to purchase the dance, the visitors stay from nine to twenty-one days in order to teach the dance (including its songs, drum rhythms, style of clothing, rituals, and magical formulas). The purchase is based upon the expectation that a local troupe will be able to learn the dance and, in turn, sell it elsewhere. However, the exchange situation cannot be comprehended exclusively in terms of monetary profit and loss, for social and cultural relationships (e.g., prestige) are being transacted and negotiated on many different levels.[7]

*Political science* is concerned with decisions and the power to make them.[8] Employing this broad definition, the political scientist can contribute to the understanding of dance at two basic levels. First, it is possible to learn more about decision-making which affects dancing. Who decides such details as which persons will participate and what dances will be performed? What are the bases of such decisions? In my own research in Ubakala, the influential members of the clan insisted that several prestigious (for non-dance reasons) dancing teams perform and be photographed if other more skillful dance teams were also to be studied. Thus dance performance was based upon artistic and non-artistic factors.[9] Second, dance can be viewed in relation to the larger political system. Such a perspective directs attention, for example, to political socialization by local and national dance troupes. A prime illustration comes from China, where the national company regularly performs politicized dances in order to impress the audiences with the message involved, whether it be the greatness of the current leadership or the evils of American "imperialism." National dance troupes in Africa are less politicized, but some clearly contribute to national integration.[10] Dance has even been introduced, for this purpose, into the armed forces. The Commander of the Uganda Army and Air Force told the men of one of his battalions that traditional dances helped to bring together all the tribes into one united nation:

[7] James Fernandez, "Dance Exchange in Western Equatorial Africa," paper read at the Seventh International Congress of Anthropological and Ethnological Sciences, Moscow, 1964.

[8] Harold D. Lasswell & Abraham Kaplan, *Power and Society: A Framework for Political Inquiry* (New Haven: Yale University Press, 1950), pp. 74-75. But David Easton, in *A Systems Analysis of Political Life* (New York: John Wiley & Sons, 1965), argues that the proper subject of political science is the authoritative allocation of values.

[9] Hanna & Hanna, *op. cit., passim.*

[10] Judith Lynne Hanna & William John Hanna, "Heart Beat of Africa," *African Arts*, I, No. 3 (1968), 42-45, 85.

Such dances allowed members of tribes to get to know each other, and everyone, including civil servants, police, prisons, civilians and politicians should participate towards the common goal. Such cultural and social activities brought the taxpayer and the security forces closer together in a common appreciation of each other.[11]

## CONTRIBUTIONS TO DANCE IN THEATER AND EDUCATION

The escalated understanding of dance which comes from the social sciences' contributions is important to theater and to education. If the process of theatrical dance is conceptualized to include composition, production, performance, and observation, the social sciences can make a significant impact upon each element. *The choreographer* is given new thematic materials and greater insight into movement vocabularies, both of which heighten the imaginative processes of image-making. Knowledge that pair dances were often performed in ancient Rome may provide creative inspiration; and the contextual understanding that such pair dances as the saltarello were often performed for erotic purposes is a significant addition to the choreographer's resources. *The producer* is aided in the theatrical presentation of dance, new or ancient, by comprehending why space should be restricted or unlimited, why costumes should be special or general, why the setting should be day or night. *The performer* can understand movements and themes of familiar artistic styles as well as the unfamiliar idioms of different times and cultures. This enables him "to bring 'truth' to his performance"[12] by providing the equivalent of the background study an actor often engages in to capture and project the essential dynamics of a particular historical period, culture, or personality type.[13] *The observer* can be expected to increase his enjoyment of a dance performance to the extent that he has an awareness of its context. Just as a listener's enjoyment of Beethoven's Sixth Symphony may be enhanced by understanding its "program," so the observer's enjoyment of an Ubakala women's dance is enhanced by knowing that the joys of birth and continued life are being expressed.

The social sciences also contribute to the various aspects of educative dance: educational administration, research discovery, classroom instruction, and classroom learning. For *the administrator* and his associates who are professionally involved in dance, the social sciences contribute to the development of dance as a recognized and respected discipline in the university (as well as an integral part of elementary and secondary school curricula). Even though an increasing number of universities have dance departments, dance specialists are not listed as such in the National Science Foundation's Register of Sci-

[11] "Dances Should Be Retained," *Uganda Argus,* March 18, 1968, p. 5.

[12] William Bales, *et al.,* "Appendix B, Work-Group Reports: Movement," in *Impulse 1968: Dance—A Projection for the Future,* p. 142.

[13] Cf. Judith Lynne Hanna, "Field Research in African Dance: Opportunities and Utilities," *Ethnomusicology,* XII (1968), 101-06.

entific and Technical Personnel; those in other arts, such as music, are listed. Yet, as Hoselitz points out, the formation of a discipline is related to three conditions:

> The first is the existence and recognition of a set of new problems which attract the attention of several investigators. The second is the collection of a sufficient number of data which will permit the elaboration of generalizations wide enough in scope to point up the common features of the problems under investigation. The third condition is the attainment of official or institutional recognition of the new discipline.[14]

Knowledge of the findings of social science, and of its methods and theories, helps the administrator to prepare and interpret reports on dance curricula, teaching methods, and the like, and therefore provides the basis for improved administrative rationality. *The researcher* benefits from social science research because science is a cumulative process that increases comprehension by drawing upon the incremental gains of many investigators. The history of the natural sciences during the first two-thirds of the twentieth century has illustrated dramatically how knowledge accumulation snowballs as each step forward multiplies later possibilities. For *the teacher,* the social sciences provide contextual materials and understandings which can enhance his ability to communicate meaningfully to his students. And the communication of dance meanings may be especially important if Philip Phenix is right in arguing (as he does elsewhere in this book) that the dance has a "pivotal role" in education as a "preparation or conditioner for participation in all of the other arts." Finally, *the student* is aided in his dance activities and appreciation by the understanding which social science context provides. In addition, dance in such context can give him a valuable cross-cultural experience. Educational impact is clearly magnified, when one is performing certain dances of the Australian aborigines, by realizing that their orientation is magico-religious and their purpose to bring food and rain in a hostile environment. Furthermore, the student's curiosity may be stimulated, leading him to learn more about the aborigines and their dances.

## CONCLUSION

Dance can be viewed impressionistically or scientifically and as a product or a process. The special province of the social sciences is to study dance—a panhuman trait—primarily as a process involving human behavior. Each of the individual disciplines can provide new contextual understanding of dance, benefiting dance theater and dance education. Thus the fusion of sciences and art further escalates man's vision.

[14] Bert F. Hoselitz, "The Social Sciences in the Last Two Hundred Years," in Hoselitz (ed.), *A Reader's Guide to the Social Sciences* (Glencoe, Ill.: The Free Press, 1959), p. 16.

# 5

## Dance for the Kinetic Generation

### by Harriet Berg

"Kinetic" is the word, it seems, for the revolution taking place in the arts of the late twentieth century; we have kinetic sculpture, mobiles, action painting, action films. These express a life-style dominated by cars, planes, and electrical impulses. "On the move," both internally and externally, is the image of a younger generation which has grown up totally immersed in a rapid-transit society.

Adults who are concerned with planning and developing educational and recreational environments that will speak to the young need to be aware of and sensitive to their kinetic needs. These needs are and always have been basic to all human beings. Our own time gives them special urgency and relevance.

Those adults concerned with meaningful curricula have a powerful, if little known, ally in contemporary American dance. For contemporary dance, born of rebellion, maturing in discipline, and constantly exploring new movement directions, is an ideal multidimensional art for today's kinetic generation.

Dance as an art in the past several hundred years in Western culture has suffered and endured enormous shifts in social and aesthetic importance. Its unique development in twentieth-century America makes this art particularly suited to a generation that is restlessly seeking new solutions to life in a mechanized society. Modern dance, born of the rebellious spirit of San Francisco's Isadora Duncan in the early 1900's, continued to ask new aesthetic questions throughout the twenties and thirties. New uses for choreography, new meaning for movement vocabulary, were demonstrated by illustrious American artists: the Denishawns, Martha Graham, Doris Humphrey, José Limón. Today a third generation of modern dancers—Merce Cunningham, Paul Taylor, Alwin Nikolais, Anne Sokolow—has extended dance into previously unexplored areas of expression and techniques, areas that vitally affect films, theater, and television as well as the visual arts.

Our young people have grown up seeing and knowing a great deal about dance. Social dancing at its most energetic plays an important role in their own subculture. It is now time for educators to plan to have every young person participate regularly in dance as an educational, therapeutic, and (finally) artistic activity.

Contemporary dance is creative. It permits—nay, insists—that each individual involve himself in the making of the dance form. Contemporary dance, properly taught, poses problems: Here . . . is emptiness; here . . . is the human body; here . . . are the elements of dance, space, time, energy. Speak! Dance speaks in the language known to all from birth: movement. It may speak dramatically, emotionally, abstractly, but it speaks above all directly, helping one to communicate directly with other human beings in this most human of all the arts. In the process of discovering the answers to movement problems, whether in a group or as an individual, whether as a student of improvisation or as a gifted choreographer, one answers some of the unanswerable questions. Who am I? What am I? How and why do I belong with my fellow man? These are the very questions with which the kinetic generation is concerned.


There are many continua from the dance of the past that contemporary dance carries into the future. Discipline is among these. The body in order to speak eloquently must be able to move with strength, flexibility, and control. Contemporary dance begins with the movement of daily life, of familiar gesture, and aspires to be more than ordinary. The body is capable of an astonishing and delightful range of movement that daily life does not begin to exploit. The discipline of dance technique opens the door for this range of movement to each person who participates. To jump—more easily; to leap—more smoothly; to stretch—more easily; to turn, to fall, to reach with confidence and ease: these are some of the challenges that give special meaning to the disciplines of dance training. Properly presented, properly sequenced, these disciplines become exciting, meaningful challenges for the kinetic generation.

Many observers of urban life note that what we most lack, in our citified existence, is daring and adventure to satisfy that love for the unknown lurking in all of us but especially in the young. The creative and technical demands of dance make dance a land of unknown promises.

In its long history as mother of all the arts, dance has often been used for magical purposes. The magic for today lies in the very real sense of immediate aliveness that the dance participant feels. The whole self is involved; one sweats, breathes heavily, feels the heart beat, senses the muscles strain and stretch at the same time the imagination is straining and stretching. How else can one be so intensely aware that he is a living creature sharing with others the splendid sensations that distinguish the living from the dead? Although achieving the mastery of an artist takes years of arduous work, even the novice in dance senses the "here and now" gratification.

The kinetic generation paradoxically spends a great deal of time, in and out of school, sitting. Words and pictures become substitutes for direct experience; the book and the television are vital components of our lives that we cannot and will not eliminate from our existence. They have a tendency to reduce personal sensory awareness to symbolic, second hand experience. Our capacity for perception, for intuitive grasping, is blunted or untapped, just as our range for movement is diminished by mechanization. Dance can help restore a more humane balance in the lives of young people.

Educators planning to include dance in its rightful place in the curriculum must ask some critical questions. Is dance still considered a "frill" in your community? Is it tacked on if and when there is room or time? Many communities will need a carefully planned program of excellent lectures, films, and concerts enabling the development of a better understanding of the values of dance. Good dance programs, like good science or good music programs, require fine staffs and adequate facilities. Then young people can be given daily opportunity in a clean, clear space to discover their movement potential under expert guidance and instruction. Dance that is planned into the core of learning can act as a catalyst, as a Promethean spark, and as an integration of many disciplines—including the other arts, the sciences, and the Three R's.

Dance properly understood may be used as therapy, as recreation, or as a disciplined art. It can be utilized as tool, as process, or as product in the education of a fully integrated totally alive human animal.

Educators must make concerted efforts, however, to change their own and the public's attitude about dance as an effeminate activity, inappropriate for "all-American" males. Too many young men have been denied this legitimate and satisfying channel for their physical and psychological development. Dance is an ideal method for building physical skills of balance, endurance, and control, while at the same time avoiding many of the overcompetitive, sometimes destructive elements that concentration on sports too often entails. Dance can and should be taught as a manly art, recognizing that the male of the species has the same right as his female counterpart to explore the full gamut of human emotion and movement qualities.

In the Indian figure of Shiva, the Dancing God, is symbolized the crisis of today. In the fire of destruction, Shiva dances the creation of a new universe. Building and dancing are the primary essentials of life, and dancing came first. If indeed we are to witness the building of a more humane society (even on the ashes of the old), dance must play its unique part in that building.

PART

# III

# Developing Curricula in the Arts

We may now proceed from the assumption that dance is an established art form occupying a legitimate place in society. It is time to discuss the possibilities of establishing dance in education. Chapter 6 explores the artist's and educator's perceptions of themselves and each other, and attempts to formulate a common meeting ground for constructive action.

Curriculum development is one means of bridging the gap between art form and educational establishment. Chapter 7 presents a process for the delicate task of curriculum development in the arts, using dance as an example. The process preserves the essence of the art and presents it in a useful manner, applicable in the school situation.

# 6

# Artist and Educator:
# A Dialogue

## by Martin Haberman and Tobie Meisel

Dialogue between artist and educator is frequent, but communication is almost nonexistent. In order to explain this, it is necessary to touch on issues sensitive to both groups. The complexity of the problem requires a non-judgemental approach to making the most objective analysis possible in presenting the perceptions of artist and educator. Hopefully such analysis will also lead to constructive suggestions for establishing the genuine communication necessary for developing school programs in the arts.

In order that a culture may be perpetuated, social institutions must be established which transmit the values and ideas critical to that society. At the same time, these same institutions must prepare individuals to cope with change, the only "constant" of tomorrow. Unfortunately, the educator is bound by reality factors: cost, personnel, facilities, significant differences in student ability and cultural background. As if these built-in requirements were not enough, the educator inherits a traditional curriculum which he must justify to a variety of professional and lay pressure groups. These may include the taxpayers' association, special interest groups (ethnic, political, religious), and content specialists (in math, science, reading) who derive their support from university scholars.

The educator is forced to believe—and to defend the belief—that we already know what to teach, that it is just a question of doing better what we are already doing. This is a natural outcome of constantly having to justify specific objectives, procedures, and evaluation measures. The educator, then, becomes a predictor of precisely who will learn what, measured by which criteria. And the press of this situation inevitably leads him into the role of transmitter of culture, rather than reshaper of it.

The artist is concerned with describing culture through his distinctive media, but he is not content with transmitting these descriptions. He constantly seeks to transcend the tradition, making new forms from the destruction and rebuilding of existing ones. This process, so basic to the arts, defies the educational practice that seeks to predict and control student responses.

To the artist, creativity is internally motivated, spontaneous, idiosyncratic, and not subject to external judgement. Skills and techniques are never beyond improvement, but they must not be concentrated on at the risk of losing the ability to create. The creation of art can only come about in a non-judgemental, stimulating environment under the guidance of those who have struggled with similar problems. The pressure for all artists is to maintain freedom from entanglements in order to stay fresh, observant, and original to create. Some artists can never be a part of the educational system.

This chapter presents a dialogue, between educator (teacher or administrator) and artist (teacher or performer), about dance in education. Following each section, we offer recommendations suggesting possible ways to transform the dialogue into communication, which in turn should lead to constructive action.

## SCHEDULING

EDUCATOR: In order to ensure that children have rich educational experiences, equal time must be provided for all children to engage in all subject matters. Of necessity, use of space, personnel, and facilities must be clearly defined. Unfortunately, the arts don't fit neatly into the curriculum package.

ARTIST: Creativity cannot be relegated to specific times in the day and in given amounts. The arts must be diffused throughout the day, using a variety of subject matters as stimuli for dance activities. The need to seize the teachable moment militates against scheduling.

*Basis for communication:* A compromise might be effected between artist and educator if scheduling of pupil activities can include "givens" and "choices." Most educators and artists will agree that pupils should have some part in determining a portion of each day's work if only in order to capitalize on motivation. Specific blocks of time could be designated for all activities, including the arts. At other times, students should be free to self-select particular activities for study in greater depth. This would facilitate planning for the educator, provide arts as a part of the total curriculum, and ensure time for the interested child to pursue more intensely that area of the arts with which he is most concerned.

## PRIORITIES

EDUCATOR: School traditionally emphasizes social studies, language arts, science, and mathematics. In addition, it emphasizes factual rather than perceptual forms of knowledge. Not only are the arts as subject matter secondary, but any way of knowing which is cognitively rather than affectively oriented is and must be emphasized. It is not necessary to reiterate the shopworn issues of curriculum priorities.

ARTIST:     If the school is traditionally oriented, the arts, particularly dance (which has always been basic to man and his civilization), should occupy a prominent place in the curriculum. While some artists are concerned with this classical rationale, all are concerned with preparing the individual for the future. This preparation requires emphasis on the problem-solving approach and the awakening and heightening of the senses to counteract an increasingly dehumanized society. Unfortunately, dancers have minimal bases for pressuring for their interests, since they are a small unorganized lobby in the university and community.

*Basis for communication:* Improvement of instruction and learning in the arts demands that educational values be made more consistent with society. The current resurgence of interest in the arts seems to provide the educator with a chance to reflect social demands and, at the same time, help to fashion and mold public taste.

Artists should recognize that in a technological society their art will not occupy the central place in the curriculum. However, they can expect it to be an integral part of the curriculum, with tangible support in the way of resources, personnel, and facilities.

Forward-looking universities are equating the value of achievement in the arts with that of achievement in other disciplines. There is no reason why elementary and secondary schools should not also provide opportunities for achievement in the arts. Further, the ideal of a liberal education implies broad experience in many areas; and according to what is now known about child development, the various experiences should have equal priority at the elementary as well as the university level.

## CLIMATE

EDUCATOR:   Schools are group operations maintained by control, order, and respect. The unpredictable expression of emotion is a threat to the system, displacing control and order. Compounding this fact, the body is the instrument for emotional expression in dance. The climate of the school is organized to deal with people on a rational, less personal basis.

ARTIST:     Institutional pressures are detrimental to the fostering of creativity. These pressures are inherent in the traditional student-teacher relationship. This is not to deny that many teachers establish excellent rapport with students, but merely to underscore the basic nature of the school as a normative institution where children are taught "right and wrong," "good and bad." The creative atmosphere can never be hierarchical, since true emotional expression implies complete trust. The teacher must be not an authority but a guide. Teacher and pupil, in dancing, have one common workbook—the body.

*Basis for communication:* Creating a climate conducive to learning in the arts requires a separate area used exclusively for free expression. The place in which an activity is conducted is critical to its character. While artists must recognize that space is at a premium in most schools, and that free expression of emotion works against the smooth functioning of the school, educators must be aware that for the teaching of certain subjects there are special requirements.

While the total school environment cannot be disrupted, separate areas can be reserved for the arts. A room used for activities which inhibit affective responses in one period cannot be used for fostering free self-expression in the next. In a separate room designated for the purpose, the artist has the best chance to create an atmosphere for eliciting open creative responses. At the same time, this special room becomes a sub-environment, not impinging on the order of the total school environment.

Another special requirement is clothing, particularly in dance. Of course, there can be no debate about the need for appropriate attire for any activity.

## EVALUATION

EDUCATOR:   The need to process students through the system demands clear objectives and judgemental (objective or subjective) assessments. Whether teachers compare students to themselves, to others, or to preconceived standards, all school activities are undergirded by a hidden agenda—judgemental external evaluation.

ARTIST:       Artists, and in particular dancers (whose medium is non-verbal), have developed a useful language for communicating among themselves. This advantage often works to their disadvantage in communicating with educators. Artists think in terms of exploration and internal states of being, not readily observable responses. To the artist there is no single acceptable response to any stimulus. Often there is an overreaction on the part of artists to anything resembling a highly organized educational program. Many who teach the arts, fostering creativity, when confronted by the educator take the position that creativity cannot be taught. The teaching artist, though aware of the educational objectives that structure his dance program, is reluctant to specify them.

*Basis for communication:* Evaluation in the arts must be open-ended and account for unanticipated as well as predictable responses. The fact remains that educators need some criteria with which to gauge progress and thereby justify the existence of their programs. While artists have their own criteria for assessment, they balk when asked to make them explicit in educational terms. Their reluctance derives from the belief that such specificity inhibits and leads to conformity in teaching. Artists may be correct in expressing caution about the effects of poor teaching. At the same time, they are the only ones who, by developing intrinsically valid criteria, can preclude the imposition by non-artists of inappropriate evaluative measures. Moreover, the exposition of objectives by the artist would enable him to evaluate his own dance program in terms of progress toward those objectives.

It is reasonable to expect educators to accept valid criteria derived from the discipline and to expect artists to develop the criteria for justifying their programs to those outside their field. Such criteria, for judging individual student progress, are needed not for grading purposes but to form the basis for continual assessment and revision of the instructional program.

## CREDENTIALS

EDUCATOR: One way of ensuring quality of instruction is the reviewing of credentials. These are usually college credits and the completion of state certification requirements. In the absence of clear, agreed-upon ways of assessing instruction, educators have been forced to deal with these indirect criteria.

ARTIST: Many artists have sacrificed formal education for a performing career. In many cases, a performing career is relatively short, and dance instruction is often a natural sequitur. Artists argue that experience is equivalent to written credentials or college certification.

*Basis for communication:* Certification of teachers should be based on experience, performance, and pupils' learning, not entirely on transcripts and records. Universities have a responsibility to clarify the competencies of teachers and to develop programs of certification in the arts. For the many artists who by-pass the usual preparation for teaching, certification offices must be willing to accept not merely experience as such, but experience plus demonstrated competence in actual classroom situations. Further, artists can, through working with teachers, help them to reach greater numbers of children and to transform bad art activities into good ones, good art activities into better ones.

# 7

# The Positive Use of Conflict
# in Curriculum Development

## by Martin Haberman and Tobie Meisel

The authors have been involved in a unique curriculum development project. The impetus for the work came from a university professor more interested in child development than in a particular content field. The idea was then passed on to an educational research laboratory funded federally through the Office of Education. The staff, which included no teachers, supervisors, or experts in the content areas, was charged to develop curricula in the arts for children between the ages of three and eight. At the time we terminated our connection with it, the project had produced the beginnings of an excellent dance curriculum, a methodology for its further development, and a research design for its field testing. We cannot here describe the curriculum itself; however, it was interesting for us and may prove helpful to the reader to analyze our approach to curriculum development and the process—the positive use of conflict—which emerged.

Who initiates curriculum development? The usual way is to involve teachers, supervisors, and experts, with one of the three groups providing the initial impetus. For example, a group of teachers, recognizing the difficulty of having to cover too much material in one area of the curriculum, may form a committee to condense and intensify the material. Supervisors sometimes spend the summer revising curriculum in their special areas. In a few dramatic instances, in certain areas of math and science, subject matter experts have perceived a need for more than revision, and have introduced a whole new approach to the study of their discipline.

In the literature of curriculum development, cooperation is assumed to be the basic process. In practice, it is more common to find one of the like-minded groups mentioned above dictating a specific approach in a content area. For example, we can predict that teachers revising a given curriculum have certain common concerns: There is too much to cover. How do we select the most important ideas? How do we insure that the content is equally distributed according to grade level? How can we be expected to cover the same content with children of different abilities?

Where supervisors, teachers, and experts are involved together, it is usually separately and in sequence, with one group having the power to dictate to the others. For example, supervisors frequently develop a new program, then hire consultants they know will agree with their point of view, and then get lip-service agreement or seeming compliance from teachers. Thus, it seems to us that present conceptions of cooperation can be ruled out as the basic process of curriculum development. If a group of like-minded persons are involved in a curriculum development project, their needs and perceptions of the critical problem issues are identical; if dissimilar groups are involved, their apparent cooperation masks the power play. In both cases "cooperation" is an inappropriate term.

The basic assumption of the process we worked out is that no group trumps another, that dissimilar groups—experts in dance, child-development people, teachers, behaviorists, and administrators—all contribute, but on a non-sequential, non-status basis. The diagram below shows what we perceive this process to be. The perimeter of the wheel indicates that all five kinds of experts are continually engaged in producing and criticizing their own and others' ideas. The hub and spokes indicate that a central team bears the responsibility for producing synthesis out of the conflict that would ensue if these groups were expected to develop productive ideas through direct cooperation.

One key element in this process is that the members of the synthesizing team must be discriminating generalists, able to consume and interrelate the products of the expert groups. The second critical element is the designation of responsibility to this synthesizing team for the actual product.

What is positive conflict and how did it emerge? We began by naively inviting representatives from the five groups depicted on the model to a summer conference. After being "locked up" for six weeks, we thought, they would emerge a unified group, with common objectives, mutual perceptions, and a curriculum in dance. Cooperating becomes the basic human need if one faces the prospect of living six weeks with people communicating on different levels about different things. To fulfill their need to cooperate, participants reached a superficial level of generalization which prevented them from getting to the specifics. Such a process is designed to foster practice in the art of diplomacy rather than the nurturance of thinking. Because of this factor of personal accommodation, no pecking order emerged to the extent that any one group was able to sell its frame of reference to the others. Consequently, no one came up with a product.

At this point the synthesizing team took over. To develop the raw materials into a curriculum, the process followed was to keep individual consultants apart and to consult with them on a separate but concurrent basis.. Our new assumption was that conflict of ideas is inevitable, and that the paralytic cooperation produced by their direct confrontation could and should be avoided. The positive use of conflict is desirable and possible in this context.

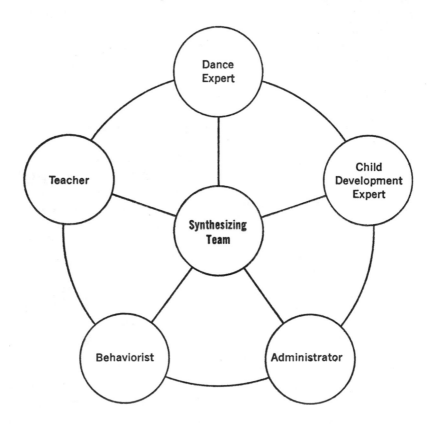

Consultants were not allowed, either within or between groups, to face one another and drift into amiable but superficial cooperation. Further, they were allowed neither to break into open warfare with one another, destroying the dialogue, nor to express their ideas in discrete fragments without the benefit of each others' criticisms. Instead, through the process of feeding their ideas through the synthesizing team, their conflicts were kept in continuous contention. This enables a dispassionate but responsible synthesizing team, serving as generalists, to keep the dialogue open and constantly expose each consultant's thinking to other forms of expertise.

Obviously the advice of experts cannot be accepted *in toto*. Each consultant will probably offer advice relating to the total situation, not limiting himself to his particular specialization; for example, a dancer may discuss research problems, and a researcher may pass judgement on an art form. Also, even within their own fields, consultants frequently give bad advice. The synthesizing team must assume responsibility for checking out doubtful advice with others in the consultant's own field, and for judging the appropriateness of advice offered by consultants on matters outside their expertise. To state it simply: the team must know whom to ask for what, when.

Evaluation of an existing curriculum can also be based on the positive use of conflict. The synthesizing team should limit each consultant to his specialization. They should consult dancers for judgements about what youngsters should learn in dance and for criteria for assessing dance achievement. Guidelines for specifying instructional intentions and for evaluating student changes should be sought from behaviorists. From child-development people, advice should be requested about the most appropriate stage for learning given material. From administrators, advice should be confined to recommendations concerning dissemination, teacher-training, and implementation. And from teachers, advice on instructional methods, field testing, and evaluation should be solicited.

The essence of our approach to curriculum development is this three-part assumption: that different people have different things to offer; that these offerings will not naturally mesh; and that a vehicle must be created for combining contending ideas into a productive outcome. Synthesis—the positive use of conflict—is the process which enables a productive outcome.

# IV

# *Dance in*
# *Higher Education*

Perhaps the university is the logical place to begin improving attitudes, practices, and preparation in the field of dance. While most college students are exposed to art and music, dance is largely neglected. If society is to benefit from and appreciate the important contributions of dance, it must be included in the general college curriculum. Virginia Moomaw discusses this and related issues, including the controversial question of where to locate the dance department in the university.

The university is the center of extensive research for almost every specialized field of study except dance. Yet dance is not only an art form to be experienced, but also an art form to be studied; and the results of such studies can often be applied in practical ways. Patricia Rowe offers a thoroughgoing examination of scholarship in dance and comments on research that has been completed and research that should be initiated.

Nancy Smith's article raises other questions relating

to the scope of dance in the university—the preparation of the performer and choreographer for a professional career. Traditionally this training has come from private instruction. Can and should the university dance department share in this function? If so, how?

Given that dance has intrinsic value for all, it must also be offered in our elementary and secondary schools. To make available effective and qualified teachers, either an expansion of teacher education in the arts should be effected to include experience in dance, or teacher certification in the arts must be instituted. Gene Wenner offers practical and specific recommendations for dealing with this problem.

# 8

# Dance in the
# College Curriculum

## by Virginia Moomaw

The notion of dance in the academic setting is strange to many people, alarming to some, appropriate to a few. The "few" are rapidly increasing in number. The "many," when they hear the word *dance,* are likely to think immediately of the June Taylor dancers or the Rockettes—of entertainment dance. They think of dance as something light and frothy, or as amazing stunts of balance and skill that hold the attention for a moment's laugh or cheer. This kind of dance has little to contribute to the cultural development of an era, or to the cultural development of an individual. The "many" might also think of social dance—of the latest "thing" in the discotheques, or an old favorite such as the waltz. Much social dance is forgotten after a few months, but some evolves into a new pattern or, like the waltz, makes a contribution to dance as an art form. The greatest value of the social forms of dance is social involvement.

To the scholarly mind wrapped in traditions inherited from medieval institutions, only that knowledge which can be precisely stated, examined, dissected, and carefully documented is the subject of true scholarship. This kind of scholar is alarmed at what he calls "lowering of standards" when a university offers courses in non-discursive subjects. To him a course in any art, especially dance, is alarming. He feels that, in a relaxed mood, one might indulge in the enjoyment of a poem or essay, but that the intangible will-o'-the-wisp stuff called art should never be offered toward the fulfillment of degree requirements in a respectable university.

Considering that advanced sciences and mathematics are theoretical, we must recognize that the academic world, in its search for meaning and knowledge, is in fact dealing not only with rational comprehension and concepts supported by well-documented facts, but, more and more, with intuitive and non-verbal knowledges gained by sensitivity and perception. As accepted disciplines began to employ creative activity, as well as experimental and exploratory techniques, the arts began to gain recognition as another area where creativity was indicative of maturity and a high level of ability. The creative act is now viewed as a universal mode of human activity. That is, the creative act may occur in any medium or academic discipline, and is always basically the same kind of process, requiring the same kinds of psychological and mental activity.

Anthropologists tell us that dance is performed by most of the peoples of the world. Dance has been used for every purpose and need of man. Religion was the main motivation for dance until the flowering of European courtly life; and it motivated much dance activity even later. It seems to this writer that most of the world's religions have been concerned with man's reason for being, with his place in the universal pattern. Why is man here—for what purpose? What should he do, and how, to fulfill that purpose? Since dance is motivated by the universal concerns of religion, man in dancing becomes completely unified, spiritually and physically, and is also discovering and perceiving his uniqueness and his value.

Today's society finds a great need for art; we value art highly. The enjoyment and practice of art is today's "quiet place" to which we return from the ceaseless bombardment of the senses, the continuing and conflicting demands, in order to refresh ourselves and find order and meaning in our daily living. Art as an enrichment and as an expression of the human spirit is a great need of the individual and of mankind.


The goal of the university is the same as that of the arts: to understand the purposes and fulfill the needs of man. The academic world has maintained excellence in scholarship which today is broadened to include most areas of human interest, including the arts. A requirement of the doctoral degree is a work which makes a contribution to man's knowledge or development. Such a contribution can now be non-verbal, as in the arts, or verbal, as in the traditional dissertation. The world of the alarmed scholar was first invaded, perhaps, by writers of fiction and poetry, soon afterwards by musicians and painters, later by drama, and more recently by dancers. This invasion has changed the university; and it has also changed the arts—and the artist.

The old idea of the conservatory of the arts has given way with the development of the arts in the academic curriculum. The picture of the starving artist in the attic is changed. Today's artist may be in a picket line. He does not try to survive as a genius waiting to be discovered; he tries to find his special place in his art and the place of art in the society. Today's artist needs not only to know his own medium extremely well but also to know something about the other arts and the larger world that he inhabits. He becomes a businessman in the market of originality and talent rather than in stocks and produce. He must know his market as well as his product. His publicity must be as good as that of other businessmen. He figures his income and expenses, and pays income tax. A university provides contacts with other arts and opportunities to learn about many things such as political patterns and scientific techniques that may affect or may be utilized in art media. A college faculty usually represents a variety of points of view and backgrounds. A conservatory is more likely to expound one point of view; it often stresses the development of ability to perform in a pre-set pattern or style. The university usually wishes to expose the student to a variety of styles and patterns and to develop individual style.

The university of today is a complex structure which tries to offer each student a challenging and valuable curriculum which fulfills his particular needs. This goal is sought in spite of increased enrollments and a mushrooming body of knowledge which must somehow be reduced to courses and curricula which can be presented in a flexible pattern and yet provide depth. The scientist, the historian—those in disciplines other than the arts—are now required to take courses outside their chosen field with the intention of fulfilling the needs of personal enrichment.

No matter what discipline the student chooses for a major, he should have an opportunity to do work in the arts, including dance. He should have the opportunity to learn by experience why dance has occupied such an important place in our culture. A course in dance may bring him the satisfaction of working creatively, expand his awareness of the world, and provide new insights about himself and his interests. The feeling of well-being may be gained from meaningful exhilarating movements. A student should gain an understanding of what dance is as an art form and how it differs as such from dance as entertainment, social exercise, religious ritual, or therapy. He should, through experiencing dance, develop a discerning eye, so that he can recognize good movement and appreciate a good performance. He should have an opportunity to study choreography, to learn to recognize good choreography, and to be intolerant of poor choreography. Students should become good audiences. After graduation they should do what they can to ensure that good performances are brought to their home communities. They should also seek out and support dance teachers of merit for their children and their cities. Dance courses should be a part of the humanities requirements of the university. These courses can be organized in many stimulating ways—on the basis of anthropological studies, structural forms, theories, historical periods such as classical and romantic, aesthetic appreciation, and so forth. The humanities-oriented courses are the more easily accepted by the academic mind. These are often the best means of informing both students and faculty that dance is a serious and important art.

Until the past few years, dance has usually been a part of the physical education department for women. This is the one department which has felt that dance was important enough to employ a teacher so that courses could be offered. If this department also believes in a liberal education for everyone, dance is usually taught as an art. Then its value and contributions to the curriculum and to the student are great. If it is taught as something else, dance usually degenerates into a fitness program. Dance is now becoming recognized as an art form which is a discipline with its own body of knowledge. Whether dance is a separate department, or a department in the school of fine arts, or a department in the school of health, physical education, and recreation is of less importance than its recognition as an entity needing to work out its own goals and objectives. Dance needs to obtain the curricula, scheduling, staffing, and facilities needed to fulfill its goals and objectives. The dance department needs to have policies regarding performances, tours, and public relations patterned to its peculiar needs. The first "few" who thought dance belonged in the academic setting, the people in physical education, were followed by a few more who saw it as a means of enhancing their productions of opera or drama. With the recent development of dance as an independent art which is leading the other arts into a new aesthetic exploration of form and meaning, it will no longer be held back. The dancers are now among the "few," in terms of the total college faculty, who see independent needs and goals for dance in higher education. Some physical education and some fine arts faculty see these needs. The group must grow larger.

The general faculty and the public should not have to be reminded over and over of the existence of dance. When the scholarships are awarded in the fine arts, or funds are granted, the dance department is left usually to say "Me too! How about dance?" Scholarships are not available to dancers via the physical education department.

Yet there are some advantages to including dance in the department of physical education. Students can elect dance who might otherwise not take time to do so. Dance is not in competition with other activities in terms of performers or technical staff needed. The football team suffers no loss of ticket sales even if the dance company is performing that same evening. There is no conflict in scheduling, no competition for publicity.

Dance in the department of drama or the department of music may be subordinated to the host art. It may be difficult to maintain an independent point of view. If the music department prefers Bach to Bernstein, the dance may be restricted to classical ballet, or at least made to emphasize it. Dance curriculum development may be restricted. Dance in the school of fine arts may encounter problems in connection with the scheduling and staffing of performances. On the other hand, the school of fine arts which is developing all the arts can offer important advantages. The dance student needs contacts with the other arts; he needs to exchange ideas with students in the other arts. Various problems such as long hours of rehearsal are common to all the performing arts. Longer class hours and much practice time is a common pattern instead of an unusual one. The need for performances, touring, and flexibility is a common problem which would be helped by academic understanding. The combined strength of all the arts is needed in seeking adjustments to these problems.

It is necessary that dance in the university be recognized and supported as an independent art, an academic discipline with a specific body of knowledge. It should have as its goal excellence in dance as an art in whichever way it is used. It may be developed into a number of career curricula or lead to higher degrees. Degrees with specialization in dance should be made available on all levels. Dance should be used to supplement and to support other disciplines to the degree it is possible. And for each student, dance opportunities should be provided for enriching experiences and discovery of his own value.

# 9

# Advanced Studies in Dance: Theory and Research

## by Patricia A. Rowe

Perhaps one of the last realizations that come to mind as we observe an expert in action in the performing arts is the extent and depth of discipline that led to his absolute ease of execution. Though the art of the dance may seem to be entirely physical, unlike dramatic art which requires the memorization and projection of the spoken word as well as some physical sensitivity, dance requires a fine balance of emotional and intellectual controls as well. Dance as an art form is being given its due recognition in more and more colleges and universities throughout the United States as a subject worthy of advanced study for itself and not as an adjunct to long-established programs of study. The scope of the discipline referred to earlier becomes increasingly apparent as we see how enormous is each year's expansion of knowledge and how the rapidity of change directly affects the total life of man. Inasmuch as no single factor can be pointed to as the reason why increased numbers of individuals are seeking both baccalaureate and advanced degrees, it seems advisable to examine probable reasons for the increased interest in scholarship on the part of dancers.

To begin with, there are more trained dancers in this country than ever before in history; and the number of college students, undergraduate and graduate, is greater as well. Although it would be logical to simply assume that this means there are more dancers than ever before who have completed college degrees, no known facts and figures can be quoted here to corroborate the logic. It is a fact, however, that the total numbers of separate dance departments and of undergraduate and graduate dance majors has increased considerably throughout the country during the past decade. From their heavy concentration on the teaching of dance, all levels of graduate programs in dance have begun an inevitable expansion into allied and adjunctive interests—related arts, dance therapy, dance history and philosophy, writing and criticism for dance, performance, choreography, dance notation, and various kinds of research, including field research. Later on, this proliferation will creep back into undergraduate curricula as the size, staff, and facilities of the given university warrant such specialization.

Perhaps also the tempo, complexities, and uncertainties of the times are making the academic discipline a more plausible partner to the dancer's readily acceptable disciplining of his physical being. In truth, the required combined disciplining of mind and body (an idea as old as the record of Greek civilization) is harder today than it was for the Greeks. In theory, the development of the whole individual is required for dance—the disciplining of mind and body must go jointly. In the past there have been unusual individuals whose natural wisdom allowed them to self-educate their minds while concentrating on the development of their own dance form. It seems needlessly difficult for today's young dancer to attempt the self-education of his mind in isolation from other human beings after his junior or senior year in high school. Though it is undoubtedly true that the dancer's body can be fully prepared for dance without a college background, that future dancer or choreographer is a product of what he knows and what he was exposed to in literature, in the humanities, and in the sciences. Just as the body can grow unresponsive and toneless from disuse, so can the mind grow dull, slow, and careless. Thus, a concentration on the development of the body alone in preparation for a career in dance becomes a questionable decision. The futility of such a choice may not become evident until a period in the individual's life in which it is too painful to risk the failures that might be involved in acquiring the verbal and intellectual skills required for the combined discipline of mind and body.

On the other hand, the teen-ager who takes advantage of the storehouse of knowledge open to him through high school and college, and of the concomitant critical discussions with informed peers and faculty, can experience —at a vital turning point in his growth—some finesse in locating, acquiring, criticizing, and valuing knowledge, with a breadth of interest in the known and to-be-discovered world. For the dance performer these experiences in mental discipline can keep mind and inspiration alive during and out of periods of dancing. Thereby, as an undergraduate, he gains curiosity, along with some knowledge of history, understanding of the relatedness of the behavioral sciences and the liberal arts to his own art form, and faith in his abilities to call upon basic skills in the language arts to supplement the communicative skill being gained in dance. Thus, and regardless of his choice of undergraduate major, his combined disciplining of mind and body contribute to his future potentialities as a graduate scholar.

Albeit undergraduate major programs in dance are increasing at a rapid rate, a predictable lag exists between graduate programs of the present in which a majority of applicants were not dance majors and those of the future in which the case will be reversed. Two major problems of graduate programs in dance are occasioned by the fact that students applying throughout the 1960's did not necessarily earn their baccalaureate degrees in dance: (1) Whereas such a student is well worth the risk as a dance major, he faces the necessity of making up a variety of undergraduate prerequisites, depending upon his previous dance experience and past major. (2) The student's undergraduate major is frequently a determinant of the nature of the theory and research he can pursue for his master's or doctor's degree.

For example, the substantial list of undergraduate prerequisites for someone with a private school and ballet background frequently includes modern dance technique and composition, biological and physical sciences, and mathematics —and education courses if he intends to teach dance in public or private schools. The physical education major may lack breadth and depth in all dance courses including performance and composition, music, dance history and philosophy, and the liberal arts; whereas the liberal arts major may need all of the education requirements for teaching, or may have to make up requirements in anatomy, physiology, kinesiology, and ethnic forms of dance.

Following or concurrent with the completion of such prerequisites, the graduate major in dance goes on to complete about 36 credits for an A.M. or M.S. or M.F.A. degree, and about 54 additional credits for an Ed.D. or Ph.D. degree.

In doctoral dance programs, a dissertation that makes an original contribution to knowledge is required. A written thesis is also required for a master's degree in many programs that prepare dance students for college teaching (the requirement being justified by its emphasis on the written language that college academia has traditionally expected of its faculty). A thesis of this type states a hypothesis concerning a problem in dance, describes the testing of same through appropriate research methods, analyzes results, and proposes conclusions regarding the original hypothesis. However, there are three recognized variations of the written thesis requirement in specific universities: original choreography that is staged and performed; original choreography that is performed and Labanotated; and original choreography that is filmed as a permanent record.

The requirements of discipline and scholarship in research are the following: (1) the analysis and clear statement of a felt need for research, from which will stem (2) the formulation of unanswered hypotheses, (3) the building of research methodology, and (4) that degree of internal consistency which makes possible the systematic repetition of methods and forms in future knowledge-building processes.

People who have or are able to absorb a broad knowledge from unpublished literature are much needed in all realms of dance to contribute to a logically devised system of theoretical model-building for research. University and separate research centers are needed that are willing to specialize in one or two areas of dance research—areas such as history, learning and movement education, "danceology," curriculum planning and development, dance as a performing or creative art, and philosophy of dance through the ages. Thus, with the right kind of climate for sharing and discussing conceptualizations with individuals who have the broad knowledge referred to earlier, and with centralized information on numerous topics of study, students should learn faster and contribute to findings in their area of dance.

A splendid example of this kind of effective collaboration is provided in the book *Folk Dance Progressions,* by Lidster and Tamburini.[1] Whereas the book title is the same as that of a valuable little pamphlet by Lucile Czarnowski, the Lidster–Tamburini book does what few recent texts in dance have done; it has absorbed the best of what was in the pamphlet and gone on with its own analysis and synthesis of certain ethnic dance information to add to the reader's knowledge of ethnic relationships. It does this by recognizing the best earlier sources in the four cultural areas chosen—Balkan, Israeli, Philippine, and Scandinavian. Each area section of the text was written by one or more persons who had studied, traveled, or lived in the area. In addition, the authors provide background evidence related to the numerous primary sources used in formulating ethnic interpretations and in synthesizing facts concerning the relatedness of dance step patterns.

The really difficult problems that face the full-time researcher in dance are, in many ways, the same ones that face highly trained researchers in the behavioral sciences (including physical education) and the visual and performing arts. Studies dealing with evaluation, teaching, and learning in the affective realm continue to be difficult. It becomes increasingly apparent that there are few hard-and-fast facts related to the process of education that have grown out of experimental research in education.[2] While dance research is still naive in this type of study, it would do well to heed the precautions of those who, like Robert Ebel, question the value of many efforts to add to knowledge about teaching through so-called basic research—research which attempts to arrive at the establishment of a system of concepts and relations that have proved, under appropriate testing, to be statistically significant as predictors of similar specific conditions.

Dance researchers who plan experimental studies of the non-natural phases

---

[1] Miriam D. Lidster & Dorothy H. Tamburini, *Folk Dance Progressions* (Belmont, Calif.: Wadsworth Publishing Co., 1965).

[2] Tom Lamke, "Introduction," *Review of Educational Research,* XXV, No. 3 (1955), 192; and George Mouly, *The Science of Educational Research* (New York: American Book Co., 1963), pp. 429-76.

of formal education should certainly heed Ebel's warning to psychological researchers: "The 'variables' we ordinarily work with in education—such constructs as ability, motivation, success, environment, self-concept, etc.—are so global and encompass such a diversity of specifics as to defy precise definition and exact quantification."[3] Ebel points out, furthermore, that learning is a natural phenomenon and that empirical data, discussion, and consensus through reasoning are valid tools that should not be overlooked in the attempt to be "scientific" above all.

Psychologist Gardner Murphy corroborates Ebel's views on basic versus applied research. In discussing the scientifically questionable reports of certain parapsychologists, Murphy has stated that it is not the experimental method per se that makes psychology a science; rather it is the "intelligible system of events" that constitutes the science. The experimental method "must fit into a cosmic frame."[4]

Though dance researchers still naively look in from outside on many complexities of the problem just discussed, they have already walked into one booby trap that catches too many research psychologists—the use of inadequately formulated questionnaires and surveys for inadequately understood purposes. Rather than following the sociologists' exemplary understanding of the questionnaire and the survey as invaluable sources of facts for further analysis (even of hypothetical cause-and-effect relationships), dance researchers seem to prefer to follow in the footsteps of psychologists, whose use of these tools has thus far seldom been worth while. A score of questionnaires and surveys have crossed this writer's desk in the past five years; as sources of data for master's and doctoral theses, their shortcomings were quite obvious. Many of these have reflected insufficient faculty sanction and guidance to compensate for textbooks (in psychological research) that fail to give adequate criteria for choice of problem, sampling of population, structure and design of questions, and form of analysis to be used on data gathered. Yet a poorly constructed question begets a loosely structured and inconsistent set of responses—if respondents take the time to answer it at all.

Dancers are turning to these two research tools more and more as they seek an understanding of the rightful place of advanced study in dance (in all its forms and aspects) in the total university and in divisional and departmental structures. As a consequence, it behooves dance researchers to heed the warnings of knowledgeable psychologists to look to sociological guidelines for help in this area.[5]

---

[3] Robert L. Ebel, "Some Limitations of Basic Research in Education," *Phi Delta Kappan,* XLIX, No. 2 (1967), 82.

[4] Gardner Murphy, "Parapsychology—New Neighbor or Unwelcome Guest?" *Psychology Today,* I, No. 12 (1968), 55.

[5] Sam Sieber, "Survey Research in Education: The Case of the Misconstrued Technique," *Phi Delta Kappan,* XXIX, No. 5 (1968), 273-76.

The gamut of subject areas that indices of research in dance include closely resembles that of the areas offered in undergraduate dance courses and of the specialization areas for advanced work in dance. Topics relative to teaching problems and practices touch on the different kinds of dance (from rhythms to dance as a performing art), on levels of learning and of schooling, and on evaluation—usually in the form of tests and measurements. Topics related to more general knowledge include history, philosophy and aesthetics, related arts, and relevant sciences.

Dance researchers have yet to take full advantage of the information to be gleaned from studies that have been conducted not in departments of dance or physical education but in other departments sufficiently sympathetic to the values of dance to sponsor dance-related research. In a considerable number of instances, the sponsorship of such studies in universities has taken place well ahead of the present trend toward autonomous dance departments. Many of the dissertations so sponsored (despite the inclusion of some variation of the word *dance* in many of their titles) are not noted in *Compilation of Dance Research 1901-1964* (the most used index of dance research listings for that period). A quick survey of the dance titles found in F. J. Litton's comprehensive listings of dissertations on theater provides a typical example of this point. For just 22 such dissertations, relating specifically to theater and dance and completed between 1920 and 1964 but not listed in the *Compilation,* there were 8 different sponsoring departments within the hosting universities. None of these departments was a dance or physical education department; 6 of the dissertations were in Music, 5 in Fine Arts, 3 in Anthropology, 3 in Romance Languages, 2 in Speech and Drama, and 1 each in History, Education, and English.

An additional proliferation of presently unpublicized dance research appears in the area of field research. Global programs such as the Peace Corps, International Exchange Programs for Teachers, student fellowship programs for study in foreign countries, research programs in anthropology and other fields are gradually adding to personal and departmental storehouses of data on or related to dance. There are potential gold mines of resources such as ethnic films of the less-frequented regions of the world, personal slide collections illustrating costumes and topography, and oral histories of renowned personages who have contributed to the development of the aesthetics and history of dance.

To properly establish the study of dance on a suitably advanced level, we need to initiate action and analysis in a variety of areas:

1. Truly and undeniably we are unaware of the range and depth of the research that has already been done in dance and related fields. Well-trained fact-finders—students who want to learn about research, interested librarians,

studio artists who want to keep their minds active and informed about dance, dance historians, many others—are sorely needed to search out this information. The very first step in its use and application is to locate and identify it —by author, title, subject, vintage, availability, and location—so that others who are trained to envision the possible relevancy of bits of unrelated facts to a bigger whole can expend their energies in the interpretation, further analysis, and synthesis of data from newly discovered sources.

2. New methodologies for using data need to be developed in order to retain, in some valid and reliable form, the facts and fictions associated with their collection—a record of the researchers' viewpoint in gathering and interpreting his materials—for use by future interpreters. For example, there are two sets of truths to be found in the field study of the same tribal dances as recorded by two different researchers: first, by a student previously trained in longitudinal research, who then lives in each country for a year or more filming indigenous dances; second, by the peripatetic film recorder of the dances of half-a-dozen tribes within a three-month period. They should be looking for different things, and their interpretations should bear out different observations as accompaniments to their films.

3. Re-examinations are needed of the source materials upon which rest many of our historical facts and theories about dance. We need to formulate and test new hypotheses concerning the degree to which certain "facts" or theories were based on circumstantial or empirical evidence, or were a result of intuitive conjecture, or are still plausible theories of interpretation. Although certain authors may have been recognized scholars of their time, the limitations imposed on their interpretations by insufficiency of available data in some areas can rightfully lead to questions whose answers may simply depend upon altering old conclusions in light of new findings based on assessments of both old and new findings.

4. The whole concept of dance history as a college subject needs revitalization. Too often its contents are restricted to what is required for the edification of dance major students.

5. In too few places do dance appreciation courses have a place among the required humanities course choices for all students. Much experimentation needs to be done to present the appreciations of art, dance, music, and drama in their philosophical and historical relationships.

6. Experimental evidence need not be confined to university studios. Students and non-university personnel, when trained to use the appropriate means of collecting data, could do so with permission and guidance in specific schools and professional dance studios. In the areas of speed and quality of learning and technical skill alone, much evidence could be gathered relative to such variables as the dancer's body build, temperament, and length and power of concentration.

So it is that the dancer's practice of combined mental and physical discipline may bring him back to college for additional learnings required for progress in specialized dance fields. Dance in advanced studies stands on the threshold of a new era of maturity. This point and one other are the major messages to be gleaned from an amazing number of conferences held during the past four years among dance educators, writers, critics, performers, choreographers, school administrators, and others interested in physical education and in the fine and creative arts. The second major point is that it is high time for dancers to cast aside any squirrel-like tendencies they may have toward hoarding knowledge. Only by sharing thoughts and hypothesizing about all phases of dance knowledge is it possible to undertake the necessary replication of once-tried experimental studies. What has been tried needs to be made known. By pooling similar findings for joint analysis and decision-making, credence can be given to a growing body of knowledge in dance. By working together, new and old higher education programs for dance can gain and maintain the standards that will give dance its rightful, unique place among the developmental, creative, and performing arts.

# 10

# Dance in College:
# Performance and Choreography

## by Nancy W. Smith

> But do not
> Flatter yourself that discipline and devotion
> Have wrought the miracle: they have only allowed it.
>
> C. DAY LEWIS[1]

It has long been a commonplace that academe has not provided the most fertile soil for the nurture of the artist, that the real world of authentic experience for an artist is not located among the Gothic spires of the university, that "institutionalized" learning poses a threat to the development of artistic potency. Dancers—the last to enter the ivied precincts—have been perhaps most fearful of the dangers. They might trip on the ivy of administrative bureaucracy, inert curricula, sterile procedures; the pavane tempo of the academic procession seemed too restrictive.

Past institutional patterns—and some present ones—have perpetrated and perpetuated these anxieties. As with other artists, the young dancer found that the exigencies of academic life allowed too little time or energy to *do the thing* called dance, to experience it, to *make* it, to *dance.* He found sometimes an almost exclusive concern with studying *about* dance, a valuable but second-hand experience not to be confused with the doing of it. It is ironic that in those very halls in which John Dewey has been venerated, the *doing* has often been minimized.

At its very worst, the university environment has produced "armchair dance teachers" and prospective audiences for whom dance would always be a kind of cultural cosmetic, but very few dancers.

At its best, this environment has ignited some gifted students who sought

---

[1] From "Final Instructions," in *Pegasus and Other Poems,* by C. Day Lewis. (New York: Harper & Row, 1958; London: Jonathan Cape, Ltd., 1957.)

further training and became dancers, has developed some excellent teaching talent among those who had the sensibilities and acquired the training of the artist, and has catalyzed a growing public appetite and receptivity for dance that feeds directly into what is happening to the art today.

The case against the past needs no further elaboration. The university context, *as it was,* obviously did not provide abundant opportunity for the preparation of performers and choreographers. On the other hand, there has also been some similar and equally destructive rigidity and isolation on the part of the artists themselves. Ivory-towerism has not been restricted to academic institutions. Practicing artists have at times been guilty of the hothouse-flower syndrome ("Don't breathe on my art, it might die"). This specious cultism not only produces deprived human beings but is also harmful to the art itself; it can sterilize it. Insularity is an anachronism in this day of McLuhan. The cloister for the training of a dancer can produce fantastic dancing machines, but does it often produce artists? Unfortunate examples of the cloistered context can be found both in academic institutions and in professional studios.

There is only one way to become a dancer and that is by dancing. But there are augmentations by which one becomes a better dancer and by which one makes better dance. These are provided by the kind of training that enables the individual to cultivate and develop all his powers. The preparation of the performer and the choreographer need no longer be restricted to any single locale; it can occur wherever viable, intensive training is available. The university environment is beginning to be one such locus.

Today's university bears about as much resemblance to the ivory tower of previous decades as Xeroxing does to carbon-paper copying. The secluded, protective campus—a surrogate incubator—is rapidly becoming a phenomenon of the past. No longer is the student insulated against the realities of the outside world. Today's student is not just the prospective recipient of the world; he is a prime maker of it. As universities become multiversities, the old curricular architecture is rapidly changing. Herein lies the hopeful potential for the university's role in the professional training of performers and choreographers. Significant parallels in other disciplines, in other arts, may be found throughout history. No longer is the university just a repository for and transmitter of culture. It is the place where new forms are made—new science, new music, new theater.

A 1966 theater conference report includes the following statement:

> Thus the colleges and universities which, for so long, were made to feel outside the mainstream of our national theatrical life, now find themselves (through a combination of economic, social, and cultural circumstances) suddenly located physically and creatively at the very heart of this movement, and in the forefront of those who are called upon to meet this challenge. Having played a vital part in creating this huge new audience, theatre educa-

tors must now play their part in helping create the means of satisfying it. In plain language, if theatre is going to meet the demand of the cultural explosion, rather than be blown up by it, the responsibility will fall in large measure on the educators, in productive alliance with the professional practitioners, to inspire and train the young of our country.[2]

Such a responsibility can only be met by a university that permits an art discipline to shape its curriculum according to the nature of the art itself.

The dance curriculum that purports to train performers and choreographers must be a fluid, multi-dimensional grouping of experiences in which the membrane between theory and practice remains sheer and permeable. First and foremost the student must dance; he must be dancing throughout the years spent in the program. He is learning as he dances; he is learning *to* dance, *about* dance, and *through* dance. This in no way deprives him of other domains of experience or knowledge. To the contrary, it becomes his center through which a broad experiential context is channeled and synthesized. It is the matrix of his perceptions through which he both apprehends and comprehends. But it is center, not periphery.

This means that rigid linear scheduling is not tenable in such a program (any more than serial thinking is in nuclear physics). Block scheduling of dance classes is of prime importance. The pattern of thirty-five minutes of technique three times a week is a scandalous but prevalent model. The student who intends to be a professional performer dances daily, with substantial time periods for instruction and for practice. Inasmuch as studio courses constitute the living center of his pursuit, the dance student is victimized if an inflexible administrative dictum assigns minimum credit for maximum hours. If ineffable, sentient human performance is not valued and accordingly recognized in curricular design, then perhaps only dance history belongs in higher education and not the art itself.

What kinds of dance technique should be included in the preparation of the dancer? Look at today's dancer; he seems to be an increasingly more versatile instrument, both in physical proficiency and in aesthetic range. It seems logical therefore that the continuous core of the university program should at least include both of the two major technical approaches that have characterized the art forms of dance in the Western world: modern (contemporary) dance and classical ballet. Training in the forms of other cultures would be an invaluable amplification, hindered only by the greater difficulty of finding excellent faculty for such purposes.

Just as there are values that are unique to the studio work of a dancer, there are those special values that accrue only in the act of performance, in theater production. There is marked increase in production opportunities on many

2 Kenneth L. Graham (ed.), "Relationships Between Educational Theatre and Professional Theatre: Actor Training in the United States," *Educational Theatre Journal,* XVIII (1966), 321.

campuses. A prime aspect of a dancer's training is the opportunity for what Stanislavski refers to as being "private in public." Ideally this should occur in varying degrees throughout the preparation of the dancer; and in this respect perhaps academic dance programs have a slight advantage over studio work alone. Opportunities to perform and audiences for performance are accessible. The crucial needs are: (1) greater variety of kinds of performance opportunity (studio recitals, workshop or experimental "lab" performances, varied audiences, full theater production, collaboration with other performing arts); and (2) excellent repertory. The fact that, with a few outstanding exceptions, most university dance programs present their own original repertory is both good and bad. It does insure that new dance—some of it quite good—is being made throughout the country. However, it is equally obvious that too few dance students have the opportunity to perform in masterworks. As dance notation becomes more refined and more widespread, and as professional artists become more and more a part of university programs, the young student dancer will have increasing opportunity to work intimately with excellent material.

Such ideal experiences, no longer totally visionary, are also central to the requisite training of the fledgling choreographer. From the beginning, he is making dance—small pieces of it at first, much that is bad, some that is good. Ideally, he performs in good material, works with good choreographers, and continues to make his own fearful trials.

Both as performer and choreographer, the dance student can be aided in handling his materials. The learning of craft, the development of proficiency, can be lubricated by skilled instruction. The miracle *cannot* be made; it can perhaps be ignited and nourished; it should, at least, be permitted. There is no such course as Divine Madness 101; but the university, as well as the private studio, *could* be a place to let it happen.

And what has usually been the igniting factor in the successful development of an artist? Hasn't it usually been the potent encounter with a master teacher, with an artist-teacher? Perhaps, then, that is the key problem of dance in higher education: acquiring a dance faculty of such artistic calibre that it serves as a lodestone for aspiring performers and choreographers. This becomes a more probable possibility, as has been demonstrated in some instances throughout the country, with the growing receptivity and understanding of the nature and value of the arts on the part of university administrations. Why would the artist come to the campus? At present, there are some obvious practical reasons, and they are similar to the reasons why some young student dancers stay on a campus for training. There is freedom from economic hardship— and most dancers have discarded the romantic myth that hunger pains beget artistic genius. (They prefer other hair shirts for the necessary artistic abrasion; hunger makes you dizzy.) There is opportunity to perform and to choreograph; there are usually audiences, and not *always* of the captive variety. There is often a decent studio and a theater facility which can be obtained with only a moderately fierce battle. There is frequently technical production assistance, and there is usually the chance for productive synergistic relationships with faculty in the other arts. And most of this abundance—thus far—is relatively union-free!

Until recently, the aforementioned benefits have had greatest appeal primarily to those artists who have begun to feel the fatigue of their endeavors in the large metropolitan centers. Even so, their relationship with the university has been for the most part mutually profitable. There is, however, a growing incidence of practicing artists and master teachers on campus who are there because they perceive valid and substantial avenues for the vigorous pursuit of their art. Academe is seeming less like the comfortable, inevitable pasture. It would seem quite likely that tomorrow's multiversity will include and attract artists because of its aesthetic energy as well as its practical advantages.

Higher education has already assumed many responsibilities—political, economic, scientific—not traditionally associated with it. The arts continue to become a more lively element in the national public consciousness. It seems a logical imperative that the university will become a catalytic force in preparing the performer and the choreographer for what José Limón has called "that lonely and aristocratic encounter."

# 11

## Teacher Education and Certification in Dance

**by Gene C. Wenner**

The present conditions for certification and teacher education in dance across the country are, at best, sporadic and confusing. Certification in dance is relegated currently to inclusion in physical education certification as a small phase of that very diverse program of studies. The presence of dance in the curriculum of the elementary and secondary schools is scarcely visible even in the gymnasium.

The need for the establishment of effective education programs in dance in the public schools is evident. But this goal cannot be accomplished without facing squarely the problem of certification. A concern with certification in the dance field as an *arts* certification has grown out of a Title V (ESEA) project to develop a secondary school course that includes art, music, dance, theater, and film. This curriculum project of Pennsylvania's Department of Public Instruction is concerned with students relating to art forms and developing effective dialogues of response to them. It was early apparent that there was a lack of teachers qualified to discuss dance as an art form and to present the student with experiences that would lead him to a better understanding of dance.

In prospect, certification of dance teachers in an arts program seemed like a simple solution to the problem, but it became apparent after some research that there was no precedent for this in any other state. A number of important questions had to be conclusively answered before such certification might be approved and put into effect. The first question was: "If teachers were certified in dance, how would they occupy their time during the school day?" Or this could be phrased differently: "Is there a need for dance teachers in a full-time teaching assignment?" These questions are both related to a broader one: "What kind of dance instruction should be provided in the elementary and secondary schools?" And still another question to be answered was: "What kind of undergraduate teacher training program would best prepare dance teachers for the public schools?"

Although these might appear to some of us to be questions with obvious answers, documentary evidence of an expressed need for dance programs and dance teachers had to be supplied by school administrators. The possibility of setting up undergraduate programs in dance education where they do not now exist was also explored.

The Commonwealth of Pennsylvania has adopted a type of certification that is called program approval. Colleges and universities who offer programs of teacher education in any subject field must have their programs evaluated over a period of years, and programs found to be of high quality are approved. The graduates of these programs are then granted automatic certification. The burden for determining the qualifications of the prospective teacher falls upon the preparing institution rather than resting in the hands of "credit counters," as it previously did and still does in many states.

In keeping with this trend, a proposal to certify arts teachers with major areas of art, music, dance, and theater is under consideration. The fields of art and music have had certification for many years, but dance and theater have not. To exemplify the degree of involvement this proposal implies, the material that answered the previously stated questions is essential.

The need for dance teachers was assessed by a questionnaire sent to the school administrators throughout the Commonwealth. It asked them for information about existing programs in dance, the need for dance in their schools, and the possibilities for adding dance teachers to their staffs in the future. The survey showed that a high percentage of administrators were in favor of the inclusion of dance or movement courses in their schools. Since many schools had had limited exposure to dance, their administrators were unable to suggest the *kind* of dance course they might favor. Although a majority of schools reacted favorably to the prospect of engaging a dance teacher if one were available, in many cases the administrator was unable to understand how such a teacher might fit into his school's program at the given time. This undoubtedly reflects a rather general lack of understanding of the potential for the involvement of dance in the total school curriculum.

There have been other significant developments that assisted the Department in suggesting the kinds of courses and time involvement a full-time dance teacher might have. The senior high school related arts course mentioned previously, which is now being pilot-tested in 70 school districts throughout the state, provides one type of involvement with dance teachers. A curriculum project in dance for the secondary schools, developed at the Philadelphia Dance Academy by Nadia Chilkovsky Nahumck, is being used in selected schools in Philadelphia. It is expected that this curriculum will be expanded for use in many school districts throughout the state. A program of creative movement for the elementary schools is also planned for the future. It is on the basis of these curriculum projects that the need for qualified dance teachers exists. A K–12 (kindergarten through twelfth grade) developmental program is envisioned that will provide broad-based content for all students as well as specialized training for the talented in dance.

Standards or guidelines for undergraduate teacher training programs in dance were developed. There is a great deal of disagreement in the dance field about what a dancer should study, and with whom. For the comprehensive dance program just described, the prospective teacher of dance must develop knowledge and skills in as many forms of dance as possible in his four-year undergraduate program. A dance teacher with knowledge and skill in ballet only—or in modern dance, or social dance, or folk dance only—would be greatly limited in a broad-based K–12 program.

An undergraduate program in dance education might have the course and credit arrangements proposed in the model shown on page 78.

It is necessary for any program to be a combination of general, professional, and specialized courses. The model program is regarded only as a general standard and not as a rigid pattern that must be used by any college or university applying for program approval. If different approaches or course structures are presented that would effectively train a teacher, their inclusion would be encouraged.

It is assumed that certification of the type proposed should in no way destroy the complementary relationship that now exists between dance and physical education. It should point the way for encouraging a teacher who wishes to explore dance as a major teaching field to pursue a program without the restraints of the requirements of a physical education program. It should also allow physical education teachers the kind of training in dance that develops teaching competence not limited, as their preparation too often is, to one area of dance, such as folk or social dancing.

The entire problem of teacher education and certification in dance is a comprehensive one that cannot be solved by attacking only one area at a time. Establishing certification in a field where there is no established need for teachers may be disastrous; the graduate may find no teaching position in the schools. When undergraduate dance programs do not include certification, the graduate is forced to take many additional hours of work in fields related only slightly, if at all, to his field of interest. To have a need for dance in the school curriculum and not be able to hire teachers for that program because of lack of certification is a serious problem for the schools. To adequately attack all of these areas, it is imperative to involve a great number of people representing many areas: representatives of the dance field, administrators, curriculum developers at state and local levels.

The problems that need to be solved first are those that must be solved

## BACCALAUREATE DEGREE PROGRAM IN DANCE EDUCATION

*General Education*

| | |
|---|---:|
| English Composition I, II | 6 |
| Social Sciences: | 9 |
| American History, European History, American Government, Sociology | |
| Sciences and Mathematics: | 9 |
| Biology, Kinesiology, Anatomy, Mathematics | |
| Humanities: | 9 |
| Literature, Art, Drama, Music | |
| Historical Survey of Dance I, II | 8 |
| Dance Ethnology | 4 |
| Health and Physical Education | 4 |
| Electives: | 11 |
| Eurhythmics, History of Music, Form and Analysis of Music, Stage Production, Aesthetics, Art History, Piano, Creative Writing, Economics | |
| Credit hours: | 60 |

*Professional Education*

| | |
|---|---:|
| Educational Psychology | 3 |
| Social Foundations of Education | 3 |
| Human Development (Child and Adolescent Psychology) | 3 |
| Materials and Methods of Dance: Elementary and Secondary | 6 |
| Student Teaching and Professional Practicum | 12 |
| Credit hours: | 27 |

*Specialization*

| | |
|---|---:|
| Principles of Composition and Improvisation I, II | 6 |
| Dance Composition I, II | 4 |
| Dance Production I, II | 4 |
| Historical Survey of Dance I, II (credit as General Ed.) | |
| Dance Ethnology (credit as General Ed.) | |
| Eurhythmics | 3 |
| Movement Analysis and Notation I, II | 8 |
| Applied Field of Performance: Dance Technique Major and Minor | 16 |
| Credit hours: | 41 |
| Total Credit hours: | 128 |

within the dance field itself. Until there is more agreement upon what should be taught in dance in the schools, and upon the kind of training that will best prepare someone to teach it, there is little hope for universal acceptance of certification. Until the acceptance of the role of dance in physical education is clarified, dance will not be a universally accepted part of the curriculum. This cannot be accomplished except by responsible persons directly involved in the field of dance. We believe we have come close to solving some of these problems in Pennsylvania, but recognize that this may not be the case in other states.

When certification for dance teachers becomes a reality, we will not allow any and every dancer who has studied with some other dancer to teach in the public schools. It will mean that each dance teacher will have had a broad training in general education, professional education, and education in all areas of dance. Certification is not the complete solution to the problem of dance in the public schools, but it will serve as an effective beginning for the development of meaningful programs in dance, from kindergarten through twelfth grade.

# V

# Dance in
# Public Education

Is it feasible to put dance as a discipline into the
schools? What will be included in the dance program? Have dance programs worked in the school
situation? What form do they take, and how successful have they been?

Elizabeth Wilson discusses school dance programs
from the curriculum director's point of view. She
deals with processes in the selection of curriculum
content and with how these involve changing societal
attitudes. Hers are practical considerations conceived
in the context of the reality of the school situation.

In Part I, Philip Phenix commented on the close
interrelationships of the arts. Rhoda Kellogg, in
Chapter 13, presents a detailed exploration of one
such relationship—one that involves the basic stuff
of dance: movement. The kinesthetic aspects of
young children's experience of art, in their spontaneous drawing and scribbling, have important implications for the total school program.

Ruth Murray, who has been instrumental in implementing a dance program in the Detroit public schools, offers insights for structuring a dance program for the elementary level. She discusses proper goals and some activities of such a program. She also comments on how dance should be taught, building upon what the child brings naturally to the experience. She suggests a means for interrelating the dance program with the other arts programs so as to provide the richest possible experience for the child.

Nadia Chilkovsky brings insight drawn from her experience as designer of an actual secondary school dance program to the task of presenting a comprehensive concept of the dance curriculum—aims, content, materials, the teacher's role, and the different ways in which all these can fit into diverse school situations.

Using the Lincoln Center Student Program as an example, William Schuman discusses another kind of educational program, concerned with audience-building and making the performing arts an alive and meaningful experience for school children. His excellent recommendations can suggest the elements of a model for developing similar programs involving cooperation between the school and any performing arts group or center.

# 12

## Problems of Balance in Curriculum Change

### by Elizabeth Wilson

My father, whose formative years spanned the two decades at the turn of the century, would have been horrified at the thought of the dance being a regular part of the general curriculum for children in the public school. Perhaps it was all right for babies in kindergarten or could be offered as a frill to polish the graces of a young woman; but as part of the basic education of any he-man: never! He was also nervous about other forms of fine art—opera, drama, symphony, art exhibits. But none surpassed the dance in its affront to his masculinity.

My father was a product of a nineteenth-century mid-American upbringing. Kentucky, his home state, prided herself upon her horses, her women, and her bourbon. This self-image was silhouetted against a backdrop of pioneer virture. Hardiness, individualism, local pride, courage, and stamina were among the most prominent. Running throughout these ideals was a persistent thread of Puritanism, nurtured by the Bible Belt and reinforced by the public school.

Curious how ego-ideals change. The Greek image of masculinity, if we are to believe Plato, was enhanced by skill in music and gymnastics. Indeed, a major part of the curriculum for the guardians of Plato's ideal state was to be gymnastics for the body and music for the mind. These studies were to nurture "high spirited, swift footed, and strong young men." We should, if we were to heed Plato's words, "observe what are the natural rhythms of a well regulated and manly life, and when we have discovered these, compel the foot and the music to suit themselves to the sense of such a life. . . ."[1]

Thus would the Greek curriculum reflect the values of Greek culture. And the American curriculum mirrors the attitudes of our society. And so, for public school children in the United States during the last hundred years, the

[1] *The Republic of Plato*, tr. by John L. Davies & David J. Vaughan (London: Macmillan & Co., 1929), pp. 107, 64, 94.

dance has not been an accepted part of the basic curriculum. Nor has it yet a well-defined place in most school systems. Many a school board member across the land feels just as my father did.

Society, however, does not stand still. Tastes grow more cosmopolitan. The performing arts are finding their way into the fabric of middle-class American life. This phenomenon has occurred not only in the "effete" East; cultural centers in such cities as Los Angeles, Dallas, and Chicago also proudly compete for artistic kudos. It is not now deemed so indecent or immoral for a young man to be interested in the dance, although a career of dancing remains outside the pale for many families.

In like manner, the dance is creeping into the curriculum—very slowly to be sure, but still perceptibly. Folk dancing, for example, has moved from being a minor art taught in far-out progressive schools into many public elementary and junior high school curricula. Only yesterday a newspaper in a large city pictured a ballet troupe performing for an admiring audience in a suburban elementary school. The caption underneath the picture noted that the troupe had a foundation grant designed to stimulate children's interest in the ballet.

Students of curriculum notice this gradual change in cultural values and its reflection in the schools. They consider the documentation of such societal phenomena to be one source of the data upon which curriculum choices and decisions should be based. The professional curriculum builder also looks for guidance toward data in two other areas: (1) the learner and the learning process; (2) the funded knowledge of mankind.

Let us first examine what we know of the learner and the learning process as a guide for including or excluding the dance in school curriculum. Every teacher who studies child development knows that there is a fundamental relation among these three factors: a child's ability to control his body with skill and grace; his feeling about himself as a learner; and the development of his intellectual processes. If we put this triangular relationship into pedagogical language, we can say that the development of psychomotor skills is intimately interwoven with the development of affective sensitivity and cognitive power. Indeed, there is growing evidence nowadays that intellectual ability finds its ground in the psychomotor and affective domains. The Swiss psychologist Jean Piaget, who has recently come into his own, postulates that sensory motor development predates concrete intellectual operations such as the learning of reading techniques.

Every good kindergarten teacher knows the value of musical–motor activity. It is only when the school becomes overly nervous about the Three R's that dancing and rhythms become "frills" or activities for "females only." Or perhaps our Puritan backgrounds reject the thought that an activity which can be so much fun and so beautiful can have anything to do with the discipline of mind and character which the schools are supposed to foster.

Yet from another viewpoint, the dance is discipline. And as it moves from its inchoate beginnings in the rhythmic patterns of a young child toward the performances required of great artists, it becomes one of the highest forms of discipline. As such, it integrates in overt ways the physical, aesthetic, and intellectual powers of man, and opens up the whole field of aesthetics as possible curriculum fare. For aesthetics *is* a legitimate field of knowledge. Jerome Bruner, we remember, brings this clearly into focus in his little book entitled *On Knowing: Essays for the Left Hand.* Art *is* a mode of knowing, he insists. In fact, Bruner is enough of an artist himself to suggest that art is the highest way of man's knowing about life. It is the concrete experience itself intensified and rarefied.

And so, if we look toward the learner and the learning process as one data source, and at the funded aesthetic knowledge of mankind as another, we find considerable evidence that the dance is more than a legitimate kind of study and activity for school children. If Piaget and his colleagues are correct, the activity may be more important for younger children than for older ones. But it is our contention that the dance should be a vital part of general education at all ages. Indeed, we Americans have been cheated of our inheritance by the failure of the public schools to offer the dance as a basic part of curriculum. Most school curricula are currently badly out of balance in this respect.

Effecting curriculum change, however, requires a great deal more than intellectual persuasion. Curriculum change of the dimension we have in mind will require attitudinal change on the part of society; for, as we have seen, our society still has considerable misgivings about art in general and the performing arts in particular. Hand in hand with societal re-education is needed a re-education of the teacher. At present, except for a few gifted people in the area of physical education, most teachers are awkward and shy about the dance. If curriculum change is to be a reality and not a dream, teachers will need to be taught as they should teach. The movement toward culture change is beginning, but it is far from fruition. It will require the efforts of a great many dedicated people, as well as additional resources, if the current imbalance in curriculum offerings is to be righted for youngsters in the schools of tomorrow.

The battle for a place in the curriculum for all students, though urgent today, will become even more imperative in the future. There is every indication that the electronic revolution will transform the school. Within the next two or three decades, it seems likely that the skill-development and information-giving functions of the school can and will be handled by electronic multimedia arrangements of one sort or another. It is possible, also, that learning of this sort will be more efficient and more thorough for everybody than it has been in the past. Accompanying this greater efficiency, however, are the impersonality and artificiality of the learning environment which creates the efficiency. To counterbalance the dehumanizing effects of such artificial environments in the school of tomorrow, the arts must come into their own and assume a major curricular role. We speak here not only of appreciation of the arts, but especially of participation, as in the performing arts. Here, the dance has a particularly important function, combining as it does several of the fine arts in an activity natural for man—whether he is to participate as amateur or professional.

Those who feel strongly that the dance belongs in today's curriculum—and even more in tomorrow's—had better begin to work now and to organize their social and political strategies. Changing the curriculum in any culture is not simple. Some wag once said that it is easier to move a cemetery than to change a curriculum! The lessons learned by the activists in the curriculum reform movement of the last decade are a case in point. Despite the amount of money available to, and the brainpower and political charisma exerted by, the curriculum reformers of recent years, there has been not much basic change in the actual practice of schools. Proponents of the dance may find that the strategy of working first with very young children can serve as an entry into some of the more hidebound sections of the school. But such proponents, if they are to make any real headway, will need to be masters of many strategies.

On the other hand, there are movements afoot which keep the present situation from being impossibly depressing. As we have seen earlier, attitudes in society do change. Such change in our cultural values, combined with more sophisticated knowledge of the curriculum process, may move the schools more quickly than we have ever hoped. Imaginative, creative individuals are already creating exciting models for those of us who wish to see, in fact as well as theory, a revolution in the curriculum. But this new vision of a more humane curriculum requires also a new vision of man and his potential. Let there be no mistake about it. Changing the curriculum does mean changing the society which generates the school.

# 13

## Movement and Mind
## in Children's Art

### by Rhoda Kellogg

This article discusses the educational significance of young children's normal movements as recorded in their scribblings and drawings. The record of these movements can tell adults a great deal about the way children see their own scribblings and develop increasing powers of perception. A twenty-year study of some 300,000 scribblings, easel paintings, and finger paintings, made by approximately 1,000 children aged 24–60 months while enrolled in nursery school, reveals data valuable to adults seeking understanding of what scribbling movements mean to the child. Understanding of these movements also enables us to see all body movements of children in more meaningful contexts.

Drawings are an excellent record of how young children perceive lines and shapes, in their own scribblings, which at a later age they observe are similar to the shapes of objects about them. I think that through better adult understanding of the origin of shaped gestalts as they develop through scribblings, educators could present the symbols of language (in any culture) in ways which would make it easier for children to become literate. With more knowledge of what development has already taken place in a child's learning of the self-made gestalts of art, the symbols of language could be introduced more appropriately. Reading lessons could be introduced on an individual basis instead of by arbitrary birth date. A child's existing knowledge of art symbols could be the basis for timing the introduction of language symbols.

Elsewhere I have presented data about typical line formation in preschool art, and about the sequential stages through which art develops from scribbles to pictures. Children teach themselves to construct line drawings acceptable to adults as pictorials of objects in the world about them by rearranging components of their non-pictorial abstract drawings. Since young children the world over draw such similar abstractions and first pictorials, there can be no doubt that biological factors account for the art of scribblings. The implications of this statement are important not only for formal education of the normal child but also for the treatment of non-typical children. Voluminous records of child art at the Phoebe A. Hearst Pre-School Learning Center are the documents which have provided the data upon which this article is based.

Theoretical Gestalt psychology, recent discoveries about brain functioning, and certain other laboratory research programs, are steadily revealing that learning experiences in the first few years of life have great effect on development of intelligence and subsequent learnings. The impact of this new knowledge on some educators has been a rush to stimulate the child's brain by sights and sounds of hardware devised by adults, tested out with "success" on a few children in laboratories, then produced by commercial concerns for mass consumption. The long-term effects of many new methods and machines will not be known for years to come and will no doubt be difficult to evaluate.

From my forty years of experience as a nursery educator and my twenty years of studying more than a million drawings done by children living in thirty different countries, I have learned much about the innate symbol system which human beings spontaneously produce in childhood. More and more I try to learn from children's natural behavior how their developing minds unfold when a minimum of adult-devised verbal and visual stimuli are pressed upon them. I am not enthusiastic about compulsory, premature teaching of abstract symbols of written language via verbalization, letter blocks, and flash cards.

Following is a brief statement in non-technical terms of how children develop perceptions and memory of the art symbols which normal spontaneous movements produce. More technical and detailed information may be found in the references listed at the end of this chapter. The total body is always involved in any given moment, all parts working in coordination under brain control of nerve impulses which control the muscles. A continuous interplay between mind and the total body integrates all movements. While in the art of scribbling the child's eye may or may not watch all the hand's movements, scribblings reveal that the child's eye does see certain gestalt effects resulting from the movements. The fact that children make duplicates and triplicates of certain scribbles shows that the eye controls hand movements toward the purpose of a visual reward.

What the retina of the eye "sees," according to Gestalt psychology, is merely millions of dots of whirling light reflected from objects in focus. It is the cortical brain which must organize these dots into meanings. Therefore seeing scribbles is a complex mental process, for both child and adult. We now know also that the young child makes scribbling movements not only for the satisfaction of flexing muscles but also for the visual stimulus his brain gets from seeing the markings on the paper. Thus, when we say something is pleasing to the eye, we really mean pleasing to the brain. One reason children's scribblings are so pleasing to them is, I think, that they are so dynamic. Like a moving picture, the gestalts change as each new mark is made, causing considerable mental activity.

The muscle movements of the hand also stimulate the area of the brain which controls hand movements. For reasons not fully known, the coordinated activity of muscle and mind achieved during drawing activity produces a feeling of well-being. To prevent children from scribbling takes the attentive effort of adults. Scribbling seems to be a satisfying body and brain activity. When done under conditions of supervision which protect them from getting into trouble, children will do a great deal of scribbling. And if they do not have paper to draw on, any smooth surface which can be marked by fingers and seen by the eye will suffice.

As for exactly what the eye sees in scribblings, Gestalt psychology says that we first see the whole, or totality, of an object, and then see details which identify it. What the eye sees as the whole is the whole gestalt; the parts are the lesser gestalts which make the whole. Whole gestalts are scribbled in great varieties, some of which are visually satisfying because of the child's placement of scribblings on sections of the paper's area. A scribbled whole gestalt can therefore be described as a *figure* on a *ground,* to use the language of art. While the details of a scribbling can also be seen as separate units, they cannot be eliminated from the vision of the whole gestalt.

Adults and children see scribbled gestalts very differently because activities of adult brain and child brain are never comparable. Differences in maturation of brain tissue and in quantity and quality of mental life result in differences in interpretations of visual data. A three-year-old will scribble a big *E* or *A* on a paper, and not see a letter of the English alphabet, as would most literate adults. These differences in interpretations of line gestalts are inevitable, and they make it necessary for adults to analyze the content of scribblings quite objectively in order to understand how the child mind works in the early stages of development in art. My taxonomical approach to child art aims at such objectivity.

I began my study of children's scribblings and drawings by grouping look-alike gestalts together and noting the age-level sequence in which various kinds of gestalts were first made. It soon became clear that all the basic graphic marks which human beings of any age can make are spontaneously made by two-year-olds. It is the combinations of these marks that determines whether a hand has produced a child's scribbling, an adult's doodling, a great artist's masterpiece, or a written message. It is the mind of the viewer which must decide. What the viewer sees depends upon his mental orientation to the material.

Normal children at age two make what I call the Basic Scribbles, which at most are twenty in number. Even at an earlier age, a hand can hold a marking instrument that records hand movement on a surface for the eye to see. Commonplace scribblings reveal that preschool children have a natural capacity for composition which I think should be described as aesthetic composition. As children we naturally teach ourselves to make movements which result in line arrangements having aesthetic shape and arrangement. There is no difference to be noted between the scribbled art of males and that of females in childhood; boys and girls have similar ability to make the basic movements and have similar retinas and brain structure. We can therefore speak of the natural aesthetic eye and brain functions of childhood.

As adults we must realize that our minds were once conditioned to believe that aesthetics and art are understood only by specialists and that children's scribblings are of little, if any, importance. Early in our school life we were painfully taught to arrive at these conclusions, and therefore adults cannot easily change their minds and agree that scribblers are natural artists.

According to my dictionary, the word *aesthetic* means "beautiful, as distinguished from the moral, and especially the useful." The shapes and compositions which two-year-olds find beautiful are also used in compositions done by the world's greatest artists, who continue to utilize forms which the human mind seems naturally to enjoy from birth to death. Each culture and era develops artists who specialize in various styles of art that become favorites with large populations, commanding regional public loyalties. Unlike adult art, child art is similar the world over, and no artist can function without utilizing its basic elements of line and structure.

To understand what kinds of gestalts children naturally scribble and enjoy we must realize that the area of the paper registers to the child's eye, with the perimeters making the most impact. Furthermore, the eye seems able to divide the paper's area into vertical, horizontal, or diagonal halves, and to see only one half as a ground for placing the scribbled figure, that is, the scribblings. The eye also directs the drawing of figures, scribblings or pictures, onto areas so that right-left, top-bottom, or over-all balance often results.

The various placement of figures on the paper's ground I have called Placement Patterns, and they are clearly discernible in the work of young children from age two. A significant aspect of some scribblings and Patterns is that in *over-all appearance* they imply outlined shapes. Those which are so shaped probably register best in the child's mind, while others are "lost" to memory, because of the nature of gestalt vision. In any case the child is able at age three to draw six noteworthy shapes in large outline forms which I have called Diagrams. The Diagrams are these: (1) circles or ovals, (2) squares or rectangles, (3) triangles, (4) odd shapes, (5) an upright cross and (6) a diagonal cross. Once the Diagrams are clear in his mind, the child combines them into abstract designs, many adorned with scribblings. Thereafter come first drawings of pictorials which we can label suns, people, buildings, animals, vehicles, trees, or flowers. At age five children who previously have had a great deal of scribbling experience can combine these items into pictorial "scenes."

As children make the shapes, the designs, and the pictorials, they seem impelled to draw them to fit into the familiar Placement Patterns which they spontaneously produced at an earlier age. As they mature, and try to draw objects which they see around them, they ignore factual shapes so that their drawings of objects will fit neatly into the familiar Patterns and outlined shapes. Children do not copy nature, as their drawings of people conclusively prove, nor do they spontaneously copy the work of adults. Instead, with the help of adults, they give pictorial labels to the various gestalts they have taught themselves to draw and have memorized. Early pictorial child art makes a poor basis for judging how the child sees the world, but it does make a good basis for evaluating capacity to construct abstract, aesthetic gestalts. Since the shapes and patterns common to child art abound in the great art of adults, we can say that all artists are dependent upon an innate aesthetic sense. "Artists are born, not made," goes the explanation of talent. Failure to realize that the child mind works with innate appreciation of form is to miss the fundamental meaning of the art of scribbling—the growth of intelligence through the mind's stimulation of movements that make art gestalts.

A universal distribution of typical child art gestalts has existed since prehistoric times, because art comes from body movements organized in ways determined by body structure and brain functioning. Only adults can chisel rocks, but even archaic man's designs did not all come out of the adult mind. Presumably nature has distributed eyes and brains as equitably in human bodies as arms and legs. It is the use to which hands, eyes, and brains are put that determines the aesthetic capacity ultimately developed by the gifted artist or the skilled technician. Many are called but few are chosen in art. Allowing children free expression of aesthetic movements is more difficult for dance than for graphic art, but both are certainly essential for wholesome development.

So powerful is the human urge and capacity for aesthetic movement that societies set up rigid controls so that individuals will conform to group activity needed to protect group life. Thus art and dance become restricted to culturally prescribed styles, with each culture preserving its own traditional restrictions. Adults teach children restricted forms of behavior in order to preserve valued traditions. Desirable as this may be, it is certainly not desirable to cut off each new generation from the innate forms of self-expression in art, as societies do when children are old enough to be formally educated.

Adults, however, think of education as pouring into children's minds what adult minds have decided they should learn. We falsely assume that, as adults, we are properly informed, when in fact we are all mental cripples in art as a result of our own education in childhood. Public education, for example, cuts children off from natural art expression by misusing graphic art, in various ways, for the teaching of subject matter. Because educators do not understand the nature of the aesthetic vision of young children, they do not capitalize on it in ways which could promote both language and art. I think the Tower of Babel story refers to the original common language of babblings and basic gestures which are similar for all children. Out of similar basic activity come the varieties of expression dictated by local cultures. Children's natural gifts for expression in art, dance, speech, and music are not adequately respected. Instead, they are denigrated as inferior to adult behavior. By not utilizing natural gifts as a basis for learning, educators add to their own difficulties.

To illustrate, most of the letters of the English language are drawn by children at age four as art gestalts, but they are not arranged in the right-left and top-bottom ways required to express language. Instead they are placed to make aesthetic composition. In our art classes for school-age children, we should point out that "letters" can be made any way we like in art, but that they must be arranged in one certain way to make writing. Children always seem pleased to know this. I think it would be worth while to experiment with having children learn to write before they learn to read, and also to have first readers printed in one script decided upon as best for the easy learning of legible handwriting. At present children have to learn several arbitrary language symbol systems: upper- and lower-case print, in various styles, manuscript, and cursive script.

When we think of the confusion and contradictions in adult minds over the origins and relative educational values of art gestalts versus language gestalts, we can understand why the school has confused pedagogical methods. It is remarkable that as many children learn to read as do, under compulsory education. Should we not take more cues for curriculum building from the natural behavior of children as evidenced by their movements and thinking in the arts?

Before the days of television and the automobile it may have been easier to teach children to read. Today their minds are so stimulated by what they see, with natural gestalt vision, that the rewards of learning ordered, non-aesthetic word gestalts are meager. First readers cannot contain very interesting content, because similar word gestalts must be presented *ad nauseam*. Thus some children can pronounce many words but fail to get their thought content in various sentence contexts unless supportive illustrations are present. I think the elimination of all illustrations from readers would be worth trying. Ditto-machine stencils and workbooks with unaesthetic adult art gestalts are probably roadblocks to learning to read. They are miserable crutches at best. By showing words only, visual stimuli are simplified and restricted to gestalts requiring the ordered eye movements needed for reading. The eye should not wander to art gestalts during reading.

We can expect increasing numbers of children to fail under the pressures of modern life unless we find methods of enabling teachers to allow more natural movement and thought to be the foundation of learning. I think that art is the royal road first to writing and then to reading. Since we cannot change the way in which eye and brain naturally comprehend gestalts, the suppression of art activities does not increase the ability of the mind to perceive letter and word gestalts in whatever linear direction the language demands. The conflict and confusion between language and art gestalts must first be eliminated in the minds of adults if children are to be spared from failure. Adult understanding of child art can be helpful in this.

That there are ordered stages of development in the comprehension of art gestalts can be seen in children's art products. Maturation based on growth seems to be a dominant factor. The statistics I present below give evidence that the child mind does indeed unfold in an ordered fashion, as Rousseau and Froebel claimed it would and should.

From numerous classifications of gestalts found in preschool work, I have made statistical counts to learn the age levels at which children first draw certain pictorial items. A first sample study (Study I) was made in 1968 of the work of 250 children who had attended Golden Gate Nursery Schools (in

## Statistical Summary of Study III

(Total Number of Children—150; Total Age Range—24-60 Months; Total Number of Drawings—33,742)

| Item | Age (in mos.) of first occurrence and number of children drawing item at that age | | Children drawing item | | Drawings of Item | | Mean age (in mos.) for first occurrence |
|---|---|---|---|---|---|---|---|
| | AGE | NUM-BER | NUM-BER | PER-CENT | NUM-BER | PER-CENT | |
| Diagrams | 28-30 | 11 | 138 | 93 | 3,322 | 10 | 37 |
| Aggregates | 28-30 | 2 | 125 | 85 | 3,960 | 12 | 39 |
| Combines | 28-30 | 3 | 121 | 81 | 1,307 | 4 | 40 |
| Learned items | 28-30 | 1 | 65 | 44 | 1,188 | 4 | 46 |
| Joined items | 34-36 | 1 | 24 | 16 | 124 | 33 | 51 |
| Suns | 28-30 | 4 | 105 | 71 | 1,045 | 3 | 41 |
| Humans | 31-33 | 6 | 85 | 57 | 2,327 | 7 | 42 |
| Vegetation | 31-33 | 1 | 31 | 21 | 170 | 53 | 47 |
| Animals | 40-42 | 3 | 28 | 19 | 155 | 46 | 50 |
| Buildings | 40-42 | 1 | 23 | 15 | 156 | 46 | 51 |
| Transportation | 37-39 | 1 | 25 | 17 | 193 | 57 | 51 |

### Mean Age (in Months) for First Occurrence of Item
### in Three Studies

| Item | Study I* | Study II | Study III | Average mean age (3 studies) |
|---|---|---|---|---|
| Suns | 43 | 42 | 41 | 42 |
| Humans | 43 | 44 | 42 | 43 |
| Vegetation | 49 | 51 | 47 | 49 |
| Animals | 48 | 51 | 50 | 50 |
| Buildings | 51 | 51 | 51 | 51 |
| Transportation | 53 | 53 | 51 | 52 |

* This study is reported in Rhoda Kellogg, *Analyzing Children's Art,* (Palo Alto, Calif.: National Press, 1969).

San Francisco) between the ages of 38 months and 44 months. Some of these children had entered at 24 months, and some left as late as 60 months. Children's ages at their first drawing of these six pictorial subjects were noted: Sun, Human, Animal, Vegetation, Building, Transportation. (These headings were found adequate for including all pictorial items made.) Three independent viewers agreed that each pictorial drawing selected was in fact a pictorial rather than a design or scribble. The percentages of children drawing the various items were determined.

A second study (Study II) was made of all other children enrolled in Golden Gate Nursery Schools from 1953 to 1967. About half of these children drew no pictorials (probably because they left school before age 44 months) or they made too few drawings (under 50) to allow judgment of their pictorial capacity. There were 109,808 drawings, made by 698 children. Since the study was concerned with age at time of first pictorial, drawings made by 54 children within a month after enrolling were omitted as not reliable examples of first efforts, making a total of 644 children in the study.

A third study of 150 children, aged 24-60 months, randomly selected, was completed in 1969. In this (Study III) the ages at which all structures and pictorials were first made were recorded. The first of the two tables includes information from Study III only. The second table compares the mean ages at which pictorials were first made in all three studies. The three different studies all show, for example, that almost a year's time elapsed between drawing of the first sun and the first item of transportation.

What the statistics mean is that, for more than 1,000 children, representing a broad spectrum of urban children from various ethnic and economic groups, interest and ability in drawing subject matter followed a definite developmental sequence.

# REFERENCES

Baker, Harry, & Kellogg, Rhoda. "A Developmental Study of Children's Scribblings." *Pediatrics,* 1967, Vol. 40, No. 3, Part 1, pp. 382-89.

Jones, Val (ed.). *Special Education in the United States.* Springfield, Ill.: Charles C. Thomas, 1967.

Kellogg, Rhoda. *Analyzing Children's Art.* Palo Alto, Calif.: National Press, 1969.

———. "The Biology of Esthetics." In *Anthology of Impulse, 1951-1966.* Brooklyn, N.Y.: Dance Horizons, 1969.

———. *Psychology of Children's Art.* Del Mar, Calif.: CRM, Inc., 1967.

———. *Finger Painting.* Coronet Instructional Films, Chicago, 1953.

*Microfiche Showing 8000 Drawings from the Rhoda Kellogg Child Art Collection.* Microcard Editions, Washington, D. C., 1967.

# 14

## Dance in Elementary Education[1]

### by Ruth Lovell Murray

People in the arts and education as well as the general public are coming to understand the meaning of the word *dance* as describing the whole body of the art. In the past, educators as well as laymen have been at fault in not giving dance its rightful name. Several years ago the term *rhythms,* or *rhythmic activities,* used to describe some of the dance activities of little children, came into favor. This was understandable inasmuch as *dance* as a word describing the total substance of dance activity was not in general use. To educators at that time, anything connected with the word *dance* meant learning dances, and therefore the term did not cover the creative use of movement in dancelike form which was beginning to find its way into the school activities of children. Because creative activity in dance was scarcely ever attempted beyond the third grade, the necessity for giving it a name at that level was not so great. Where it did occur, at least among girls, it was usually referred to as *creative dancing.*

Thus the inconsistency and confusion in terminology extended even to professional educators. *Rhythms* is a manufactured word representing only one aspect of dance expression. Whether used as camouflage or for convenience, it serves only to mislead and to deny to dance those experiences which are essential to it. A little child who moves in a precarious pattern on the living room floor to music is *doing his dance* or *dancing.* So boast his proud parents, and so actually he is; he is not *doing rhythms.* This applies to the child in school and to children everywhere.

If *dance* is to be all-inclusive, then what is *a dance?* A dance is movement put into rhythmic and spatial form, a succession of movements which start, proceed, and finish. How complex this progression must be, or how simple

[1] This chapter consists of selections, slightly adapted, from Chapters 1, 2, and 6 of *Dance in Elementary Education: A Program For Boys and Girls,* Second Edition, by Ruth Lovell Murray (New York: Harper & Row, 1963). Copyright 1953 by Harper & Row, Publishers, Incorporated. Copyright © 1963 by Ruth Lovell Murray.

it can be and still be called *a dance,* may be a point of disagreement among precise terminologists. This writer maintains that the simplest combination of movements, say only two, which a child puts together may be legitimately called *a dance.* Who can say when random experimenting with an art medium ends and expression of an idea begins: when first attempts with paint and paper are more than merely absorbing activity and become "my painting" or "my picture"; when more than one color has been introduced; when the beginning of a form is recognizable, at least to the child?

It might be said that a child who impersonates the flight of a bird or an airplane is doing a dance. To make the definition slightly more precise, let us call this *dancing* and not *a dance.* A dance is a composition, which implies an arrangement of parts into a form. Form demands contrast, even if it is only that of one part against another. Hence the child makes *a dance* if he progresses far enough in his project to have his airplane make a landing or his bird stop flying for a while and sway on a treetop or hop along the ground looking for a worm.

To use a non-dramatic illustration, a child skipping forward is dancing, for a skip is a dance step. When he adds to his forward skip a skipping turn and repeats this succession of movements, he has made the beginning of a dance. These movements may be further structured *in time* if he decides to take a certain number of skips for each part, say six skips forward and four skips turning; *in space* if he uses a high skip forward and low skip turning. Such a sequence of movements contains the beginning of formal movement structure, and on the child's level this is his dance just as much as a highly complex composition belongs to the dance artist who composed it.

While it is true that the word *dance* refers to a totality of the art, what is useful in the *dance education of children* represents only certain aspects of the whole. The great classical system of dance movement which has been traditionally called *ballet* is not included, nor is tap dance, nor modern ballroom dance. Ballet is excluded, even though a great many children receive ballet instruction outside of school, because it takes highly trained teachers, special equipment, some talent, and much practice and drill to achieve a satisfying dance experience in the use of this system of movement. The discipline which must accompany ballet training generally implies an ambition to become a performer in that field. Many children do not have this motivation; certainly most boys, in particular, do not.

Tap dance is theatrical and unchildlike, and employs highly refined and complicated foot movements. It requires balance and control which are difficult for a young child and offers little reward except the ability to perform rhythmic patterns with the feet. This is not to say that tap dance as performed by some of its great exponents cannot be very expressive or that it does not contain a certain exciting rhythmic quality. It also has the advantage of being considered more masculine than certain other kinds of dance expression. For young children, however, it is complex, is limited in expressive scope, and demands much mechanical drill for achievement.

Ballroom dance, while an important social skill for boys and girls to learn during their adolescent years, is not included because it is fundamentally an adult dance activity. Although certain folk dances use the so-called social dance position, they merely repeat the same step (such as the polka or two-step); they do not involve the free, improvisational use of steps which, in much ballroom dance, requires a close embrace or strong leading of one's partner.

Rather than being taught these specialized areas of dance, the child should learn through experimentation how he can move, how, through practice, he can move more expertly, how he can manipulate movement to discover its potential for use and for communication, and how he can build it into simple forms, thereby making symbols for expression. He should understand how to respond to the time structure of dance and should be able to adjust his own movement to it in various ways. He should learn patterns of movement which have been made by others. In this way he begins to develop a vocabulary of dance movement and an understanding of the many uses to which it can be put—for communication, for recreation, or merely to display his ability for his own pleasure and that of others.

For a child, movement is both an organic need and a constant delight. Dancing to him is good for its own sake, often without meaning or purpose. But should meaning or purpose be required, it is easily supplied by the rich imaginative resources and the unique world of childhood. If education is to become an integrated and enriching development of the total person, those experiences which involve the self in creative and constructive activities assume special significance. Dance can do this, and perhaps better than many projects with which children are involved in school. Well taught, it offers limitless potential for their sound development, for it makes expressive use of the body, the self-symbol, as does no other activity in which they engage. It can open the doors to new experiences and can add emotional intensity and meaning to old ones. It can serve as a truly recreative activity, but even more as a province of expressive and aesthetic action.

The compelling necessity is for education to use this natural love for rhythmic movement which children possess, employing it extensively to help them develop their bodies for creative uses, to supplement other learnings, and to find fun and satisfaction in worth-while day-to-day experience. Dance uses the self expressively as does no other movement activity. Human movement is one of the primary means for the communication of ideas and feelings. It should be recognized that an activity which helps to free the body of awkwardness and inhibitions, makes it more rhythmic, enables it figuratively to say to others, "Let us join hands and dance together," is worthy of a large place in the life of a child.

There are two areas which dance in elementary education should include: the movement and rhythmic components of dance, and the dances themselves, whether composed by the children or learned by them. If the dance program is to be properly integrated, these two bodies of material must be interrelated, one leading into the other and then back again. To make a dance or perform a dance may be the ultimate goal, but much satisfying activity can come from the exploration and manipulation of movement, putting familar movements into new forms, testing one's rhythmic response, and improvising ways of moving in response to imagery and to sensory and rhythmic experiences. With younger children particularly, such dance activity may conceivably constitute the bulk of the dance program. This is true because children of an early school age need to find themselves in movement before they can relate well to others, either in the making or learning of a group dance.

> A child should be helped to become aware of the wonderful potentialities of his body for movement of all kinds: to carry him through space, or around, or up and down, or out and in; to allow it to burst into great speed or to control it into slow motion; to exert immense energy into violence or to restrain it into lightness and gentleness; to stretch tall and wide with tension or to relax into the floor with loose and effortless abandon; to move a part or all of himself from one point to another in space on a straight, zig-zag or roundabout path; to crawl close to the floor or leap high to avoid it; to use his knees, his back, his shoulders, his hands as well as his feet as a base of support. The way these things feel when he makes them happen with his body will soon become a part of his general kinesthetic awareness when he moves in any way or for any reason.[2]

It is the responsibility of the teacher to make these various aspects of dance learning fit together, so that experiences are broad and comprehensive and each supports or supplements the other. All the fundamentals of dance education should be part of the dance diet of children if it is to be properly nutritious. The teacher would find it less of a task if all these experiences could be handed to her in the form of lesson sheets, with what should be taught today, tomorrow, and the next day neatly planned and ready to be handed on to the children. Fortunately, or unfortunately, this cannot be done, because communities of children differ as much from group to group in abilities and interests as individual children differ from each other.

In the early grades, programs involving the arts, and especially the performing arts of drama, music, and dance, should relate closely to each other.

[2] Ruth Lovell Murray, "Observations on the Teaching of Dance to Children," *Impulse, Annual of Contemporary Dance*, 1957, p. 2.

Experiences in one art area should spill over or lead into another. With younger children it is difficult and even undesirable to keep these art experiences in discrete compartments, to fail to take advantage of common elements in the performing arts which contribute to and reinforce each other in a full and rich performance.

An accurate movement response to aspects of rhythm should be an outcome of an integrated arts program. Some of this will be accomplished in the child's musical experiences, as more and more music teachers are using movement to develop rhythmic acuity and a feeling for the dynamic quality of music. It should be enlarged upon in the dance program, where the movement used can be more free and less inhibited than is possible elsewhere. If there are school specialists in music and dance, they should work closely together on the development of such skills in their children. If, as is more apt to be true, the classroom teacher is responsible for both programs, she should be aware of their close interrelationship and use the materials of one to support and supplement those of the other.

Another relationship to be explored more fully is that of dance to creative dramatics. The line between creative drama and creative movement with children can and should be a very thin one. The basis of this relationship is the mastery of one's own body movement and the ability to use it in a free, expressive, natural fashion. If younger children have had many opportunities to explore movement from various kinds of word images, their dramatic movement will be uninhibited and inventive. Older children identify readily in movement with favorite characters or character types encountered in their reading and in their observation of other persons. In this way, the exploitation of movement for dramatic purposes and an understanding of its communicative potential becomes a part of their direct experience. With greater maturity comes the ability to abstract specific states of feeling, emotion, or behavior and to present their counterparts in movement. This type of exploration helps a child to broaden his expressiveness in movement, whether its eventual use is for dramatic or dance performance.

In all aspects of children's movement education the problem-solving method is to be preferred. In dance, where the nuturing of creativity is of particularly great significance, much more desirable educational results are obtained through exploration, invention, discovery, than through a system of prescribed exercises, unless the latter are used for their therapeutic or remedial effect.

It is true that the learning of a dance, such as a folk dance taught by the teacher, demands imposed directions which must be followed accurately by all. Here, too, there are problems to be solved: absorbing, understanding, and reproducing new patterns built upon movement experiences that have already been explored; adapting to the movement of a partner or a group or both, so that the dance proceeds smoothly and one enjoys the sense of group unity which dancing in unison with others affords. Nevertheless there is much more to be gained by the child from his dance experiences in school than the enjoyment of these traditional patterns alone. Under wise guidance, he may invent patterns of his own which are just as beautiful and just as satisfying.

It seems obvious that movement should be one of the simplest and easiest means with which teachers may work to cultivate the highly significant creative potential in children. One can start wherever the children are and grow with them in knowledge, skill, and understanding. Freedom combined with controls and responsibilities, spontaneity with trust and respect, an expectancy that children will respond wholeheartedly to assigned tasks rather than a suspicion that they will not—this kind of environment is a wholesome and productive one for the flowering of children's creative efforts in dance.

# 15

# Dance in Secondary Education

## by Nadia Chilkovsky Nahumck

In September, 1965, when my colleagues and I undertook the task of developing a "comprehensive curriculum in dance for secondary schools,"[1] we were faced with the challenging need to select criteria for objective identification of the phenomenon of human endeavor which is called *dance*.

As the investigations progressed it became increasingly easier to formulate questions than to answer them. There were questions concerning the meaning of "comprehensiveness" in a dance curriculum, types of instructional materials to be developed, expected outcomes of the program of studies, alternative approaches to teaching techniques, value of a dance curriculum in the context of general education, and avenues to field testing in a variety of school organizations.

Early efforts to organize the curriculum along purely historical and formalistic lines were quickly abandoned since there were almost no published theories of movement, no readily available great choreographic works, and few published records to verify historic continuity.

In contrast, music theory and practice dating from pre-Christian periods can be studied directly from notations which have existed in some form since early Greek culture. Music scores available for analysis yield insight into various patterns, from the pentatonic scale and Gregorian modes to the twelve-tone scale. Diverse paintings, sculptures, and architectural works from pre-Egyptian days to the present time exist in great profusion. The development of recording and photographing technologies has made reproductions of these great works available to everyone.

Although approximately five hundred years have passed since the beginnings of modern science (with Galileo) and over two hundred years since the

[1] Development of a Comprehensive Curriculum in Dance for Secondary Schools: A University of Pennsylvania Project funded by the U. S. Office of Education, 1965-67. O.E. # H-328.

publication of the first dance notation system (Feuillet–Beauchamp), the cultural archives contain very little evidence of the choreographic works of even the renowned twentieth-century artists. Choreographies which have at least (fortunately) been notated, in Labanotation or other symbols, remain (unfortunately) unpublished. The general public is consequently unaware of their existence.

Dearth of dance literature and materials, however, has not inhibited an explosion in dance activity which is being transmitted, from artist-to-teacher-to-student-to-pupil, in a kind of "oral" tradition. In the wake of this growing interest there churns a multiplicity of extrachoreographic concerns: copyright protection for choreographic works, dance literacy among dancers, false and confusing dichotomies between "dance as a performing art" and "dance as education," assorted myths about appropriate sequence during class lessons, and the vital function in community dance involvement. Such concerns are symptomatic of a growing realization that *dance as an art should be taught by dancers who are aesthetically sensitive to its meaning and forms.* The above concerns indicate, too, the timeliness of reconsidering the value of a dance curriculum within a general education system. Dribbling a little dance in by way of an "enrichment program" is certainly not the answer. An adequate approach to educating the complete human organism involves a synergistic effort among all aspects of learning—physical, emotional, intellectual, and inspirational—in continual resolution.

This chapter presents a design rationale for the dance sector of such an educational program. The concept is graphically represented in the Diagram of a Comprehensive Dance Curriculum.

## CONCEPT OF A COMPREHENSIVE CURRICULUM

The comprehensive curriculum is conceived as a multidimensional spiral involving interweaving processes of feeling, knowing, doing, and perceiving. The shaping of these experiences depends upon recognition that dance is an art, that the instrument for dance is the human body, that the medium is movement, and that organically interlocked components of time, space, and energy are employed to design form and style structures.

The curriculum is comprehensive in (1) *scope,* (2) *range,* (3) *function,* and (4) *relevancy to general education.* It is planned to guide the student from a level of skill and understanding which he brings to his first class through a cyclical panorama of dance study during his secondary school years.

*The curriculum is comprehensive in scope,* in that it encourages the utilization of full capacities for achievement in perception and performance of dance.

To understand what is implied, one must visualize a permeating interaction of dance with other school disciplines. In the Diagram, Level I (*Exploring*

## DIAGRAM OF A COMPREHENSIVE DANCE CURRICULUM

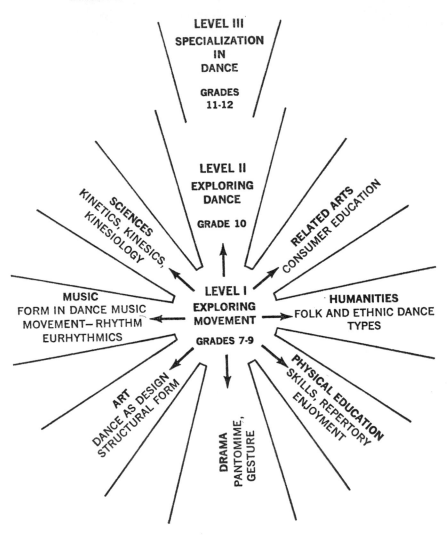

| CONTENT | MATERIALS | OBJECTIVES |
|---|---|---|
| DANCE SKILLS | DANCE SCORES | *TO RELATE—* |
| DANCE ETHNOLOGY | DANCE FILMS | THE INSTRUMENT TO THE BODY |
| MOVEMENT ANALYSIS | FILM STRIPS | DANCE TO MOVEMENT |
| CHOREOGRAPHY | TAPE RECORDINGS | THE CRAFT TO THE ART |
| RESEARCH | MUSIC SCORES | DANCE TO THE OTHER ARTS |
| AUDIENCE BUILDING | TEXTS | DANCE TO EDUCATION |
| | BIBLIOGRAPHIES | DANCE TO PEOPLE |
| | | PEOPLE TO PEOPLE |

*Movement*) is shown in reciprocal relationship to a variety of educational concerns.

The curriculum design may be imagined as a series of spirals in which the lengthening radial vector maintains continuity between the intial exposure to the curriculum concepts and the enlarging circumference in wealth of knowledge. Understanding, perception, and skill also spiral upward, creating a conical depth of accumulated learning from which the student may eventually select discrete study areas as specialized subjects. Since the learning will be cumulative from the seventh grade throughout the six-year sequence, the student who elects a dance specialization in the upper secondary school grades will have acquired a strong general foundation in the theory and practice of dance during his junior high school years. He can therefore devote himself to intensive study in performance techniques, choreography, or dance ethnology, or he may undertake research projects as preparation for subsequent study in higher educational institutions.

*The curriculum is comprehensive in range*—range of cultures, historic periods, geographic areas, dance types, forms, and styles from which the materials are culled.

Great technological advances in means of communication have facilitated information retrieval, offering new possibilities for discovering quantities of dance materials from diverse racial, religious, and national origins. These materials, arranged in developmental categories according to levels of skill required to understand and perform them, offer a student various ways to explore similarities and differences among dances of our own and other cultures.

*The curriculum is comprehensive in function,* since the curriculum plan proposes to study dance as an expression of mankind. It examines not only dance in our immediate society but also dance as ritual in tribal societies, dance as recreation, theatrical spectacle, and therapy.

A uniquely significant function of this curriculum is that of guiding the student to understand the power of his own body energy and the importance of directing it to constructive purposes. He learns to do this by understanding the structural rules (principles) according to which the components of movement are put together to form desired patterns. He learns to recognize and to interpret habituated motor patterns in his own behavior.

*The curriculum is comprehensive in its relevancy to general education.* Since dance study involves rational as well as sentient processes, it lends itself to the purposes of analysis and of imaginative "dreaming." It is therefore appropriate to include dance among the family of arts already within the scope of general education curricula.

General educational leadership has begun to take more careful cognizance of the total body as a human resource. Its capacity to receive and to transmit a continuous stream of non-verbal messages creates a perpetual soliloquy at the most intimate level.

In contrast to verbal communication, kinetic responses are freely articulated though the messages may be obscured. For the most part, they reflect conditioned physical and emotional responses at a subsurface level of articulation. Tensions revealed in the unconscious gestures that accompany discursive speech, for example, are habituated in the body. They result from repeated performance according to a pattern of psychophysical complexity in the human organism. These responses have been observed, interpreted, and redirected. Research results have been published by Rudolph Laban and his associates.

Education which aims to adjust or to integrate learning patterns in school with the motor habits the student acquires in his home and his neighborhood is especially significant when that education is focused on the total human instrument. Since this instrument (the body) is a self-contained complex of physical, emotional, intellectual, and inspirational behaviors, it needs to be educated into its cultural environment. Such education—of and through the body—is, in other words, a basic societal requirement. A *comprehensive curriculum in dance for secondary schools* is a curriculum *for all students*.

## AIMS OF THE CURRICULUM

*To teach dance as an art.* Dance, like other arts, is a combination of craft components, which provide *structure,* and of expressive elements, which reveal *meaning.* Understanding of dance as art is essential to its function as an expression of human feelings and aspirations. It is necessary for the development of a quality instrument through which the individual can express his relationship to his own universe.

*To develop understanding of dance through studying its structure and symbolism.* The universal fact about dance is that people move in selected patterns which become habituated in the body. There are various movement types. Some are perpetuated by generations of performers, without serious alteration in their gross configurations. This may be said of traditional dance types such as the European classical ballet, the East Indian bharata natya and the Scottish highland fling. Movement sequences in these dance patterns are arranged within the boundaries of codified structure. Performance techniques of such dances tend to emphasize formal design. In contrast, some other types of dance movement are designed creatively in response to immediate emotional stimuli. Such dances emphasize expression and meaning.

*To guide students in discovering their own capacities for creating kinesthetic design.* When the familiar human body assumes the role of instrument for dance, it (the body) becomes transformed into a medium for inspired, symbolic action. The most ordinary, the simplest, the easiest-to-perform motions transcend previously seen kinetic activity and seem to illuminate the weaknesses and strengths of all humanity. When the human instrument dances, all observers become participants and the audience vibrates empathically to radiations which emanate from the dancing body. Inspired dancing evokes deeply rooted human responses. These responses in turn become symbolic and inspired. Dance can invoke the creative powers, discover unexplored talents, and revitalize its own energies.

*To encourage students to draw from their own experience ideas and moods for motivating dance design.* By starting with familiar ideas, a student can learn to observe human behavior as a source of inspiration for inventive design. He also explores alternative responses to a particular stimulus and a choice of dance movements with which he can express these responses.

*To promote higher levels of taste in appreciating dance.* The development of judgement and appreciation grow from a knowledge of interacting components and principles which form the syntactical framework of the art. Increased knowledge of the dance leads to more discriminating appreciation.

*To elevate regard for the human body as an expressive instrument.* Since every human being owns a body, each one is endowed with a capacity for kinetic articulation at varying levels of conscious control. Exploring dance movement involves understanding and sensory awareness of body energy. Each student, as he becomes aware of his body's unique expressiveness, will realize some significant truths about himself:

1. The human body is universal in form and function. It is in constant and longitudinal use. It cannot, therefore, be stored away between uses as can be done with a musical instrument or with paint brushes.

2. The human body is a complex of organically intertwined sensory responses which are in constant states of change. Variations in the environment produce changes in body reaction. It has the ability to adapt its behavior patterns to a variety of conditions. Under favorable circumstances, it can demonstrate great skill and resourcefulness, which under adverse conditions may appear to be lacking. The crucial variable seems to be a *will to perform.*

3. The human body is always expressive, although the expressive patterns are not always symbolic. Bodily expression often reflects kinetic articulations which the individual cannot verbalize. Much of the kinetic symbolism is coded so that it is intelligible only to those viewers who are initiated into its meaning.

4. Dance study deals directly with the human body which serves as instrument and medium in closest possible proximity. Since there is only one body in which is vested all cognitive and affective aspects of his total learning, it is

reasonable to assume that elevating regard for the human instrument will be of advantage to the student in all his endeavors.

*To enhance ego satisfaction in girls and boys through the use of materials suitable for each gender and for both.* Dance offers the student a variety of satisfactions: physical exercise as rhythmic design; mastery of time and energy, experienced in the development of skills; self-determined and expressive use of one's effort; creative explorations involving the testing of data and skills acquired in the learning process; exercising the imagination to devise inventive design based on laws of motion, the structure of the human body, and the principles of dance design.

*To relate the meaningful self-discipline acquired in dance study to directed effort in other study areas.* Perception of the symbolic meaning in dance design can lead to increased curiosity about other aspects of human interest. A functional base line for teaching dance is scientific. It therefore relates to the logical process in science. Dance and mathematics both deal in abstract symbols. Dance and the humanities are concerned with developing a regard for linguistically and culturally diverse peoples. Dance and the other arts explore ways in which people express their attitudes toward their own culture.

## INSTRUCTIONAL LEVELS

To accommodate differences in age, capacity, skill, prior experience, and schedule complexities among the students within a school, dance study can be offered in a series of three instructional levels: introductory (*Exploring Movement*), intermediate (*Exploring Dance*), and advanced (*Specialization in Dance*). Within each of these categories, *Content* and *Materials* and *Objectives* will provide for a variety of student interests and talents—for students with great interest in dance and ability to work consistently at high intensity, for those with little interest and low concentration level, for those who learn rapidly and progress at an even pace, and so forth.

All students, for example, who have had little or no background in dance will begin at Level I. Within the stated aims of Levels II and III, materials will range in degree of difficulty so that not every student will be required to achieve the same degree of performance skill. But all students working within the scope of each learning level will progress in understanding the art of dance.

In general the learning-levels approach to curriculum organization permits great freedom and flexibility, since it can adjust to a variety of school programs. Specific objectives orient classwork at each learning level. Whether he is engaged in specific activities for developing skill or participating in dance discussion, the student's body is a medium for reciprocal flow of ideas and sensations which link dance to all other aspects of his education. During the entire six-year sequence, therefore, he learns to apply in his scientific and humanistic studies those discoveries he makes about himself in the dance classes.

## TEACHING FUNCTIONS

A good teacher is the fovea centralis of any curriculum. A teacher who is gifted in teaching and who has a knowledge of dance will be able to sort out established sequences for the presentation of classroom materials and to design the instructional strategy best suited to a particular purpose. A successful teacher will not only judge the appropriateness of class lesson procedures but will sense a need to vary them from time to time.

There are, in some schools, teachers who have had many years of private study in dance, which they have pursued as an avocation. Since dance is not yet certified for secondary school curricula, these teachers function in other subject areas when they might be used more effectively in the teaching of dance. Colleges and universities which now offer many credit courses in dance might undertake a teaching internship project which could provide secondary schools with dance teachers. Undergraduates or graduates could be encouraged to undertake work–study programs, as in other professions. Teaching assistantships, team teaching plans, student leaders, and guest teachers can be utilized advantageously in this curriculum. The important factor is the ability of the teacher to begin with a concept or an activity which is familiar to the student and guide him to discover meaning not previously perceived.

The teacher's role, then, is to provide instruction which will guide the student to discover:

1. New ways of feeling—through developing kinesthetic responses.
2. New ways of listening—by educating rhythmic responses.
3. New ways of visualizing—becoming dance-literate and acquiring dance "tools."
4. New ways of expressing himself—utilizing his dance studies to dramatize ideas and moods germane to his own life.

It is crucial to the attainment of value to the student that the dance teacher resist any tendency to become a mere imparter of data and drill commands. The teacher must function as an inspiration in the child's effort to synthesize his continuous experiences in and out of school.

# 16

# The Performing Arts
# and the Curriculum

## by William Schuman

While some educators indicate that the arts are now a fundamental part of the curriculum, my experience tells me that in the world of public education the arts are secondary. The arts are not a basic element. From the wealth of illustration I could cite to throw doubt on any comfortable reassurance that the arts are widely accepted as a basic ingredient of education, I quote from a letter I received from the Education Division of a large corporation. It informed me that a joint study that might have led to a collaboration between the corporation and Lincoln Center was being discontinued:

> The results of the research study, which was conducted by our company concerning the acceptability of a curriculum based on the performing arts, indicate widespread general interest in such a program. However, serious questions were raised regarding the ability of the school system to fit such a program into their present curriculum, due to time scheduling problems and also their ability to pay for such a program. Most teachers and curriculum advisors we contacted felt such a program might be highly desirable, but not *critical* to the development of the learner, and were most concerned lest time be subtracted from the *basic* education courses to accommodate such a new program.

Here we have a hard-headed business decision based on a most thorough research into the attitudes of educators. This research flatly contradicts any assumption that the arts are commonly held to be a fundamental part of American public education. The truth is that the field is one for pioneers, that we are working at the frontiers of education. And the truth is that the task is tough.

The reason the arts have rarely held a significant place in American public education is not difficult to explain. Public education in this country has been designed to prepare the young for the future. And that future has consistently

110

been given a vocational or practical emphasis. The primary aim of education has been to enable the young to develop skills necessary for economic security. The value of the arts with respect to this end, if considered at all, has always been thought to be tenuous and, consequently, the arts have never had a high priority among subject matters competing for educational attention.

I state this unequivocally despite all the courses and activity that educators would point to in rebuttal. I believe such neglect has short-changed our young and weakened their education. I hold that meaningful experience with the arts does help to equip a young person to deal with the problems of life, whether they be practical, moral, psychological, or spiritual.

Can anyone reasonably argue that the arts hold second place to any other discipline or learning in heightening perception, in sharpening the intellect, and in strengthening conviction? The answer is: they cannot—because the qualities which the arts offer to educators are unique; they exist in no other discipline.

The arts have suffered in the educational competition for the hour and the dollar because of the overriding reason that their nature has been misunderstood. More often than not, the arts are generally considered as avenues for emotional expression and the artist as a person who is able to express himself only in emotional terms. In consequence, educators have assigned artists the emotional provinces of man—strictly extracurricular—while the schools have been given the intellectual territory, thus creating an illogical dichotomy in which training and perception in the arts is minimized and left largely to chance while practical instruction in the intellectual disciplines is a recognized responsibility. Our blindness to the importance of the arts means that half of man's potentiality is consigned to an educational vacuum.


The discussion which follows concerns the performing arts; for they constitute the field of my professional activity. Let me mention, however, that my colleagues in the visual arts tell me that to a greater or lesser degree my convictions apply to their field as well. The first question, then, is: What is the nation now doing in the performing arts to advance the place of these arts through education for the enrichment of its citizenry? What are we doing in the performing arts in our schools and to what degree is it effective?

Presently there is an emphasis on student performances. The overwhelming majority of activity in this area takes place in the field of music, although there are some theatrical productions (usually as an offshoot of English or speech classes) and a certain amount of activity in the field of dance (usually as incidental to physical education and having more to do with calisthenics than aesthetics).

What do students get out of performing? They obviously get a great deal. They have the physical and emotional experience of live performance, of do-it-yourself psychology; and I would be the last to question the beneficial results in general developmental terms of participating in the arts of dance, theater, and music—on whatever level the ability of the student and his teacher dictates. I am not negative toward the continuation and strengthening of these group performances. Everyone knows that in their worst manifestations they are cheap examples of show business, and that at their best they constitute an approach to artistic levels of achievement and understanding. No, we need not attack in any way the concept of student performance in the schools —except to hope that the percentage at the very top will constantly expand.

The real point is that despite all the activity that has taken place in this century in our public schools, there has been little or no carry-over from these activities into a conscious understanding of the arts as the students mature. Something has been missing. Why is it that a nation which for so many decades has enjoyed expanding activities in the performing arts in its public schools has not increased the percentage of the population which values these arts?

There are a number of answers, but let me begin with the most fundamental one. A student is quite likely to go through twelve years of public school education with his entire exposure to artistic excellence in the performing arts being limited to his own performing groups and the "uplifting materials" to which he is exposed at night on his television set.

Wherever is there placed before him an example of the highest artistic standards? What can he know about the real impact of the arts unless he is exposed liberally, consistently, and persistently to the highest artistic standards of the best professionals? This is basic; but even such exposure is not the entire story.

The problem is not the stress on student performance but the assumption that those students who participate in the performing art groups in any school are getting a first-class education in those arts. The further assumption is that the other 90 per cent of the student body, those who do not participate in performing groups, do not need instruction in the arts because they have not evinced any special interest.

Classes in appreciation obviously haven't been the answer. For one thing they deal mostly in music, virtually omitting the sister arts of dance and drama, and occupy only a small part of the curriculum. Furthermore, appreciation classes are almost entirely devoid of content conceived to develop perception rather than the amassing of factual data. We are making little progress to correct this deficiency, because what we do is too little and almost entirely ineffective.

The result is that the American students coming out of the public schools are ignorant of artistic values and have not been led to the wonders of the arts through the many avenues educators have explored so brilliantly in the teaching of other subjects. All of this leads back to the fundamental problem: the lack of understanding of the arts as the basic stuff of education—as basic to the development of an educated person as mathematics, history, English, or any other content area. American public education does not recognize that if a man is callous, indifferent, and impotent in his abilities to see when he looks and to hear when he listens, he is just as deficient in the development of his God-given human potentialities as he would be if he could not read or write.

When the performing arts are presented to students, they are often treated as a form of entertainment rather than as a subject of serious thought and study. One evidence of this may be found in the fact that teachers tend to judge materials on the basis of popularity. Will the students *like* it? That is to say, if 50 per cent of the students are bored by a string quartet, the answer tends to be that there is something wrong with the string quartet, or that it is too difficult or too advanced, and that materials must be chosen to meet the least common denominator. This is regularly done with musical materials; yet English courses don't often substitute *Charley's Aunt* for *King Lear*.

There's nothing wrong with popular materials—but that doesn't get on with the business of confronting young people with civilization's creative giants. We must boldly face the need to deal seriously with our young people and not worry because great masterpieces are not always easily accessible. If the yardstick of popularity were applied to the "basic" subjects, half the population would not be able to add and subtract. And nobody would be able to spell—which is nearly the case anyway.

There is also a strange inconsistency in the attitudes of educators toward study of the arts and study in the accepted subject fields. It is assumed that a student gains by the very act of studying mathematics—that the discipline is meaningful for him even if he does not become a mathematician. It is my position that the same should be said of studying and really trying to understand the arts—that even if the student does wind up disliking what he experiences, the very effort of learning to perceive it is in itself education. This does not mean that everybody has to *like* the arts any more than they have to *like* algebra. It simply means that the arts have a basic place in everyone's education and that the *act* of *studying* them is educational.

We are only beginning to understand the inevitable and fundamental natural affinity which exists between the creative process and the educational process. If the educational process is not creative, it is boring and ineffective. And if the creative process is not educational, it is a dead end.

The implication is that all creative work has an educational goal. The nature of artistic creation is perforce educational because no work of art ever existed without a quotient of persuasion inherent in its message regardless of medium or intent. Any picture seen, play witnessed, music heard, dance observed, always constitutes an act of persuasion—an act which by its very nature educates. But the act of artistic creation need not be, and indeed rarely is, a conscious act of educating in the normal sense of the word.

The materials that have been presented by artists through the ages do provide the stuff of education in boundless measure. If, for example, we were to turn to Shakespeare for an elucidation of his political views as revealed through his plays, we could, by diverse interpretations of the characters through whom he speaks, assign almost any political predilection that we chose. The fact is that he does not educate us in specific political ideology. He educates us in diverse ways of reasoning, looking, and understanding.

Now it is easy to see this when we talk in terms of a Shakespearean character, because we are dealing with the world of specific ideas and the world of flesh and blood, albeit through the magic of the theater. Precisely the same sort of embodiment is contained in visual materials and in auditory materials. But as we listen to the unfolding of a movement of a symphony, we cannot fall back on a linguistic image to guide us. What we are faced with is something of much subtler quality.

If we really are taught to listen, we follow the unfolding of the composition as clearly as the telling of a story. What is called into play is our ability to follow a musical "story line." The last section of a movement of a standard symphony, for example, usually contains a recapitulation of materials previously heard. These materials would pass absolutely unnoticed by the listener who did not recognize that he had been previously exposed to these same ideas.

And the same criteria pertain to the dance. The unfolding of a choreographic composition which, to the untutored eye, is but a series of pleasant or unpleasant visual impressions, to the tutored eye is the progression and development of previously conceived movements toward the achievement of an artistic whole.

We have taken for granted that young people should, in the course of their education, encounter the novels of Charles Dickens and the architecture of the Greeks, but not the symphonies of Beethoven or the choreography of George Balanchine. In theater, students think of the plays of Shakespeare as something to read but not as something to watch. Why is this so? Why is it that the live performing arts are presented dead?

Certainly bringing the student to professional "live" performance can be costly and administratively inconvenient. Certainly it involves either transporting the student to the performance or bringing the performer to the student. Certainly the performing arts do not come in a neat and inexpensive package like a book.

But certainly all these obstacles can be overcome, granted one indispensable ingredient—the joint effort of artist and educator. In the past, both have been remiss. The educator has not sought or found ways to use institutions of the performing arts as a vital resource comparable to a library or a museum. And the performing arts institutions, with some notable exceptions, have made little effort to understand the needs and problems of the educator and to accord to them a high priority in their planning.

In order to give a clear picture of how at least one performing art center serves the schools in its area, let me describe specifically how the Lincoln Center Student Program works. The large number of art centers now being built from one end of our country to the other gives point to this description, for we are convinced that our experiences at Lincoln Center have significance beyond the borders of our own region.

The true performing arts center should, of course, have within it all the principal areas of music, dance, drama, and film and thus be in a position to provide the school system with a coordinated and balanced program in all of the performing arts, relieving the schools of the necessity of dealing with six or eight different institutions. Quite apart from the administrative convenience this centralization represents, the arts center and the educator working hand in hand can develop programs balanced both in artistic content and supporting instructional materials. Far from being merely a useful by-product of the performing arts center concept, this is, in my judgement, one of its fundamental and primary purposes.

At Lincoln Center we decided that the first phase of our educational program would be devoted to the secondary schools, ranging from intermediate to senior high and covering the entire gamut of private, church-related, and public schools. We also decided that it was important to develop a "two-way street" concept—that is to say, one that involved sending performing arts groups into the schools and bringing students from the schools to Lincoln Center. Both directions, I feel, are essential. The presentation of performances in the schools makes possible the exposure to the arts of the entire student population ranging all the way from those who are already predisposed towards the arts to those who have had little or no experience with the arts. The performances in the schools, too, lend a note of reality, for they make possible a personal relationship between student and professional performer and demonstrate to the student that the artists are not some mysterious creatures from another planet but men and women who have worked long years in preparing themselves for a demanding and exacting career. Then, too, performances in the schools make possible a very close relationship with the instructional program of the school and tend to remove the arts from the "field trip" or "added attraction" category.

More specifically, Lincoln Center has asked its member institutions to develop special programs designed to fit into a classroom schedule and, in terms of numbers of performers and physical requirements, into the limitations of the available high school auditorium. It is important that all performances presented in the schools maintain rigid standards of high professionalism. While it is justifiable to make compromises in terms of length of program and physical dimensions to meet special school needs, it is not justifiable to make compromises in the selection of the quality of the repertory presented or in the abilities of the artists who participate in these programs.

On the other hand, there are few, if any, schools which can house the performing arts in their full panoply; and the transportation of major performing groups to schools presents enormous problems both technical and financial. Therefore, in order to give students a chance to see these arts in their native habitat, it is important to find ways of developing the other side of the street, of bringing groups to the professional theater and concert hall. Furthermore, it is important that young people attend these performances as part of an adult audience rather than at special student concerts or student matinees. We urge schools to subscribe to a series of variegated performances rather than to single events on a hit-or-miss basis. By attending a whole series of events, a student can be given at least a glimpse of the range of the performing arts.

At Lincoln Center we are fortunate in being able to offer students in the schools of our region the New York Philharmonic, the Metropolitan Opera, the New York City Ballet, the New York City Opera Company, and the Repertory Theater of Lincoln Center. While only a great metropolitan center can support such a galaxy, it is my belief that an increasing demand for those opportunities on the part of educators will make possible a vast expansion in the number of professional performing groups. Furthermore, I doubt very much that the opportunities existing in the various communities across the country are being fully exploited.

Lincoln Center relies heavily on the active participation of individual schools in the planning and execution of its programs. For the performing arts institution itself, however eager, cannot act alone if the performing arts program is to be anything more than just another assembly period or just another field trip. We work actively with the educational community in developing appropriate study materials for use by teachers and students. These materials, prepared by artists sensitive to the needs of education, deal with the arts and do not, of course, attempt to advise the professional educator on pedagogical procedures.

One of the most important lessons we have learned is to include teachers from all the disciplines—not just the arts—and also school administrators and librarians, to give all an opportunity to experience the arts at first hand.

The most important outgrowth of this work was the decision of the Division of the Humanities and the Arts in the New York State Education Department to develop curriculum materials which will give teachers concrete and tangible techniques to use in the classroom to integrate the performing arts into the curriculum.


It seems to me, with regard to a specific curriculum in the performing arts, that there must be two central complementary elements:
1. Studies which lead to an understanding of the work of art itself.
2. Studies which lead to an understanding of the *relationship* of the work of art to the world around it.

There are many ways of approching the study of the performing arts to achieve these objectives. I will suggest two. Both are built around a carefully organized sequence of live performances representing a cross-section of the performing arts and repertories of these arts. Actual classroom activity might be variously organized, to accord with the given general approach.

One approach is the inclusion in the general curriculum of a course of study devoted exclusively to the performing arts. This would be a general exploratory course, characterized by live performances in schools or concert halls, at prearranged intervals and drawing upon the teaching staff from the various areas of specialization.

An alternative approach would be the organized infusion of the performing arts into the various areas of the curriculum in an interdisciplinary program. The entire school would devote its attention to music, dance, theater, and film periodically during the year on a unit basis, with each unit leading up to a performance in the school, attended by the entire school. Effective study of the performing arts requires actual experience with the real thing —the live product and the guidance of those who are equipped to enlighten others in the perception of the works themselves.

The arts are crucial to our automated age; they serve as a creative illumination to counteract the push-button emptiness of our mechanized life, an armor against the disillusionment and anxiety of our times, and an added defense against the destructive forces inherent in man. For educators not to grasp the vitality, the spirituality, and the intellectuality of art as central to an educated man is to ignore the measure by which our civilization will be judged.

# VI

# The Teaching of Dance

If we are to present the case for dance in education honestly, it is important that differences among those in the field be aired.

Jenny Hunter feels that dance as an art form would be compromised and diluted if taught by the non-artist in an institutionalized school atmosphere. Betty Rowen offers the view that dance can be taught effectively in the school through the use of a dance specialist supporting the classroom teacher. Ruth Dillard believes that the good classroom teacher is capable of learning and understanding the essence of dance and can provide a most effective dance experience. This is a stimulating and controversial section.

# 17

# An Artist's View of Teaching

## by Jenny Hunter

*Art is a gratuitous activity, demanding a free will and spirit, and teaching is an imposition, a necessary evil rather than an unmitigated good.*

We can't afford to forget that when we talk about teaching dance, whether in our schools or outside them, we have another art form on our hands. To ignore this fact is not only to fail to develop abilities dormant in our children but to rob them of the use of something they once had. Because we know by now that creativity, like intelligence, is present in each of us more or less, to some degree, we are concerned with the preservation of that creative ability, and we further believe that the native gift can be encouraged and developed with careful teaching. Speaking of dance specifically, we know that it can also offer an enjoyable form of "physical education" and a form of "art appreciation," but I hope and believe that the great interest now evinced in having dance available in public schools has to do most especially with its possibilities as an early, versatile, and satisfying art activity for all children—and, therefore, with its possibilities for "personality development." It happens that if we do encourage the artist-gift latent in each one of us, we are also doing one of the best things we can do for each emerging and developing personality. Those who will develop into adult artists will have had a good start, as well, since the early experience can be the same for each. But craft is more easily taught and too often confused with art; and dance in particular, with its exercises and compositional rules, lends itself to uncreative and damaging teaching. A good dance class, especially on the public school levels, should have the same characteristics as a good art class. The requirements are the same; only the elements are different.

It must be recalled that many artists in various fields—notably writers, painters, and sculptors—have insisted that public schools, from grammar schools to universities, are no place for the attempted teaching or practicing of an art, and I'm not sure I don't agree with them. Art is not something to be taught by rules, dried out by academic jargon, or dissected and judged by grading. Perhaps, if it is held that the role of schools is simply to adapt the individual to society, to condition him to unquestioning conformance to what exists, then art as a creative and individual response has no place there at all. Most of the time it is taught as if this were so. But if our role as educators ("those who lead forth") is to help our pupils discover and develop the abilities they have, so that they can feel, respond, think, decide, and act for themselves, then we shall have to re-examine what we have done in the past, on all school levels, and try to improve upon it. I must assume that, in a democracy, this last is what we really intend to do. But although this development of each person's creative ability is precisely the most valuable, the most fertile, the most rewarding thing we can hold in mind and try for, it is also the most elusive, the most easily damaged, and the most frequently ignored in teaching.

We have perfectly honorable intentions, and none of us who teaches wants to limit his students. Yet we must face that possibility. Most people are used to thinking that they can damage the young only in physical ways (since physical damage can more easily be diagnosed), and a lot of us behave, educationally, as if this were so. But as any good teacher or parent knows, other kinds of damage are possible and prevalent, though less visible.

I believe that the destruction of the creative impulse in children (and therefore in adults) is one of the most common, wasteful, and tragic kinds of damage possible, and has as its root the widespread misunderstanding (through our own miseducation) of the nature of creative growth and of art. We must begin with ourselves, since the creative impulse is either crippled by or does not survive poor teaching.


The nature of art is to change. To give a child the opportunity to develop creatively means to help him be more perceptive, more responsive, more confident of his own ability to create in his own way—in short, to realize his own freedom and right to his unique mode of expression. Some things, such as verbal expression, are like contracts between people. We agree that certain symbols shall mean certain things, and so we learn the language. We must learn to spell. But art expression isn't like that. It is not something that has to be done. It is drawn from our own feelings, and the number of common symbols is limited. The artist continually invents new symbols, which the art audience must come to understand only through its own ability to respond with its feelings. It is in the exploration by various individuals of varying modes of looking at the "real" world that the perception of all of us is expanded.

Most of the time our art classes teach only what has already happened. When art "training" is given in public schools, it tends to be taught from limited points of view related to the past, and has such early and formative importance to the pupil that eventually it tends toward the development of an "academy," or school of thought, ruling out any ways of working that are not within the artistic range of a circumscribed aesthetic (set of working rules). Our artists now, as always, feel the crippling impact of a contemporary "academy." Children taught by these academic rules grow up to be our lagging audiences, less able to appreciate the art perceptions of their own time, and they become the parents of the next generation of children, parents who, again, must be re-approached by school systems trying for more creative methods.

An artist is never "ahead of his time"; he can only be "of his time." But too often our teachers and critics are voices of the past, objecting to new viewpoints as invalid, rather than being open to new perception and experience. Strange, isn't it, to think now that Mozart was once criticized harshly for his dissonances, and that Beethoven, Isadora Duncan, Martha Graham, Cocteau, Stravinsky, and countless others, including the Impressionist painters, with whom we are now so comfortable once caused the public considerable and well-expressed discomfort? But we, too, have been conditioned by our existing art education, and to the extent that we are unable to free ourselves, we continue to do the same injustice to our artists, as audiences and as teachers, and to rob ourselves of our own unself-conscious pleasure in art.

What we need is art and dance education which, at least at first, opens the mind to possibilities and offers people the chance to explore—not education which offers only inhibiting sets of rules from the past. In dance, we must not confuse the craft with the art. We shouldn't teach only dance "steps" and "patterns." Nor should we teach only dance history, in the guise of compositional rules. These might come later, but a conceptual framework and creative freedom should be well established first, as in any other good art class.

There is a certain dynamic, or progression, involved in the natural growth of creativity. Only after a child develops freedom and a strong degree of confidence in his ability to create—and, in this case, after he has had time to explore the elements of dance—can we begin gingerly to suggest directions and possibilities, give some introduction to the movement craft (exercises to strengthen, coordinate, free the body), and point out some of the ways dances have been made in the past. When we start these things, we are endangering the existence of the creative ability which has been entrusted to us. Artists, who ought to know, keep saying this; but people seldom listen. It is a very delicate balance to maintain. We must watch each child for signs that the influence of these "rules" is becoming stronger than his own ability to originate, stronger than his confidence in the rules he makes for himself. If it seems that this is happening, we must withdraw the teaching of craft and history again, in favor of continued creative pursuit, until creativity with confidence and craft can finally be drawn along together. Only under these circumstances, I think, should we teach craft and history (or "composition"), and I think the evaluation of these circumstances is too difficult for most of our teachers. It would be better to do as one California psychologist has done (with remarkable results): simply provide the space, a rag-bag, instruments, phonograph and records, and the supervised but non-directive opportunity to do what children like to do, anyway, to move and dance. I must stress that the creative atmosphere and the opportunity are much more important than directed activity and 99 percent less damaging. To give up trying for creative work, to decide to teach only the craft, in most cases, will be to destroy the ability to create, since that ability, like any other skill, requires practice and, if not encouraged, easily retires, rarely to reappear with any strength.

The problem we have with "rules from the past" is that we tend to consider them permanent answers. We would like to feel that there is a comforting list of universal truths that will hold true for all art, but if there is, no one has yet discovered it. Change remains the only constant, as difficult as it is for us all to keep readjusting to it. Aestheticians have given us theories which momentarily defined what was happening for a particular kind of art at a particular time in history, but aside from giving our students a sense of history so that they don't, in ignorance, repeat the past, these precedents should not be made so important that they become sacrosanct rules, not to be broken. The Expression Theory of art says, in brief, that all art is done for the self-expression of the artist. The Communication Theory claims that all arts exist because people (including artists) feel a basic need to communicate with others. There are other theories, too—Art for Art's Sake, the Play Theory, Art As Experience (for the audience)—and currently still more are being developed to explain new art. The point is that each of these theories was developed *after* the fact, to "explain" art and to attempt the development of a "system" by which art can be *reproduced.* The art always happened first, out of the artist's own unique perception and expression; afterwards, the aestheticians analyzed what the artist used as rules for himself. The trouble is that though each of the theories seems to be valid in itself, none is complete enough to cover all the ways that artists now work and will want to work in the future.

Art goes through continual cycles of destroying past rules, returning to the elements and, viewing them in a fresh way, responding to them directly, then building from them something completely different. This is the essence of creative activity of any kind, and the ability to experience it is one of the most valuable and lasting skills any person can have. Thousands of mathematical puzzles now to be seen in books and magazines can only be solved by this kind of creative destruction and rebuilding. All of us once had the fresh ability to respond simply to the elements in a situation around us, but few people retain the free use of that ability.

This means, too, that what may appear chaotic in a classroom may only be part of this cycle of rediscovery and invention. No creative teacher advocates completely undisciplined behavior, but the differences required in classroom discipline may be hard for an outsider to understand. Self-discipline, after all, can only be acquired through "letting the rope out" and letting children have practice at it. The aim should be, eventually, to develop the kind of freedom with self-direction that will allow pupils not only to solve problems but to invent and pose problems of their own, as any artist or scientist does. It must be expected that this kind of profound creative and personal growth can only take place over a period of years, and one must not be satisfied with the seemingly quick but deceptive and superficial results possible with more imitative teaching.

If we could grow used to thinking of past rules only as explanations of the past and not as rules binding upon artists in the present and future, perhaps we would be closer to understanding what art is and, therefore, how to teach in it. Dancers are particularly guilty of a narrowness of scholarship concerning their field as an art. In composition classes, most of the time, they cling to compositional rules borrowed from eighteenth-century music, condemning practically everything else; yet musicians have long since gone on to other ways of organizing time and putting together sounds. Even though dancers may explore more recent ways to compose, they really feel, inside themselves, that they aren't "doing it right" if they stray too far from those first rules. They have little confidence in their own natural feeling for form because they have lost access to their own pre-conscious thought processes. People develop habits of thought about art and then believe these habits to be intrinsic truths. Because these habits are rarely consciously recognized, they are rarely examined objectively by the habitué, with the end result that the mind grows inflexible, resistant to change. If these people are teachers, the inflexibility is perpetuated.

Ways of working, freedom of attitude, self-discipline, and inner growth are all more important than any judgement of a particular art *product*. We must recall, for instance, that the Impressionist painters once had to exhibit as "The Salon of the Rejects," renting space of their own, because the French Academy would not accept their work. New art may require new crafts to be developed by the artist, and the old ways may be useless to him in the new aesthetic he has developed for himself. When an artist does accept a past aesthetic as his own, he is accepting a particular "academy" and composing within a "school" of painting, sculpture, music, or dance-making. But to a large extent, he has stopped responding directly to and interacting with his own environment and times. Someone else eventually has to break out of the mold by returning to the artist's perpetual right and obligation to his own freedom of response and expression, and only then does new art happen. It is a far greater service to our pupils to encourage them to remain responsive to their surroundings and flexible of mind and impression, so that they will be able to create new solutions to the new problems they most certainly will face.

I don't see how people can be graded on art work. This presupposes a measurable standard, against which each art product can be tried, competing for validity against other, similar forms. But we have no such standard. Only superficially does one or another set of rules seem to hold for a while. We have fallen into another habit of thought—phrasing our art criticism (a negative term to begin with!) in moral, ethical terms: "good" and "bad." This is a relic of thought left over from days when *aesthetics* as a branch of philosophy was only treated as a branch of *ethics*. In fact, no one yet, in philosophy or aesthetics, has ever found a way, once and for all, of measuring either the validity of a work of art or the progress of an artist; and it is in the field of philosophy that our most profound probing of these matters has taken place. If those who have given the most thought to the problems of art cannot agree on rules for any portion of it, then how can the school systems set up standards by which a child can be graded? When we are measuring reading comprehension, spelling, ability to sing on pitch, or the size of oranges, we are measuring tangible, comparable differences, but a teacher grading art work would necessarily have to grade by intuitive rather than objective standards (for there are none). The tests suggested to me by those interested in setting up such "practical" standards have been incredibly naive and lacking any sense of what it means to practice art. Merce Cunningham once wrote to me, "No one can tell you what to do. They might tell you what they might do, and that might make conversation."

I have found, very often, that a child I at first thought hadn't grasped something I had presented was, upon my more careful consideration, really working on it from a completely unique point of view. We simply can't always know what is going on beneath the surface, and I believe grades are damaging in art work. If we are really to learn from the past, in historical fact, we should remember how terribly wrong were those first assessments of Mozart and the others. Yet we propose to have our grammar school art teachers make assessments that artists and aestheticians wouldn't dare to make. Can't we relax the necessity for comparisons and grades in just one field? They are really provided for administrative convenience and as something to show parents; but I have always found it possible to educate the parents. One of the first things that an individual, no matter how young, must feel as he tries to work creatively, is that he does the work for himself, not for the approval of anyone else or for comparison with anyone else. He can be encouraged, but he must feel the worth of his work within himself; and to compare here is to stifle. Encouragement, itself, must be well placed, since a child will try to repeat that action for which he receives approval. If a teacher singles out a particular movement in a dance, labeling it "good," he may be faced with endless repetitions of that movement as the child tries to do again that thing which gained approval. It is far more freeing to the child when the teacher tells him that he has done something original. (Though in the traditional sense I was not her pupil, I remember Margaret H'Doubler's joyous shouts to students: "See! And you did it yourself!") Yet the pupil mustn't be urged too much, either. He must be allowed to feel comfortable with himself on those days when no ideas will come; he should not feel that he has to create. Everything should be done to promote his own relaxed confidence in himself. Many pre-adolescent and adolescent pupils have come to me already tired from the "encouragement" of their parents and teachers to "achieve," and beginning to be so fearful of not being able to measure up that they are frozen in their ability to do much of anything. (Better not to try than to fail.) The ability to work freely comes with, among other things, the conviction that one's creative work, like a gift to be given, is one's own and is always acceptable. It does not have to be done. One can only do it because one wants to.

A child learns with the first report card what grades mean. In art work, those children who don't receive the higher grades often become convinced that they are not capable of any creative work at all, and are driven away from pleasurable experience in art, rather than being encouraged to do whatever they can do, for their own pleasure. Those who do receive a good grade on art work are encouraged to do the kind of work which will again gain approval. Most of the time we place approval on the art product, rather than on the growth in the unmeasurable inner attitudes which help art activity to happen. This is the exact opposite of our stated intent and will produce imitative and repetitive rather than creative work, with less gain to the real personal growth of the student. Even if we grade for originality, we still judge by subjective standards and place pressure on the student always to be original. He can never relax.

Much, much too often, teachers in creative arts don't understand what they teach. Again and again, in my nineteen years of teaching adults and children, I've heard the story, or one like it: A little boy of six, fascinated by a water tank he has seen on a short vacation to a near-by city, builds it as his contribution to a model paper city being constructed by his second-grade class. The teacher says he can't put it into the cityscape because "it isn't square." In spite of previous evidence of a considerable creative gift, the boy is so discouraged by this one remark that not until thirty years later is the man he has become enabled, painfully and with much urging, to try his hand again at a creative art. What a tragedy. Thirty years of waste caused by one negative experience. He would have been better left alone. The creative spark is very vulnerable. It might have been possible to help him earlier, but there was no one to counteract the experience and give him back his confidence in himself. That was labeled (libeled?) an "art" class.

Adults often tell me that they "had a little modern dance" in high school or college, but decided they didn't like it, because the teacher told the class to "be a strawberry" or "be a frankfurter"—and, they say, "I didn't know how to do that." Why should they? Or they say, "The teacher gave us a problem to

make a dance in a certain way, but it was so dry I couldn't stand it." These
people have all lost the creative confidence that they once could have developed
in themselves. These teachers were inadequately prepared and had picked up
the outer forms of what a "creative" dance class looked like to them, but without understanding the real basis for creativity. They couldn't teach the creative freedom that they didn't themselves understand.

As far as professional dancers go, I find that most of the people who come
to my classes and to my dance company already having some technical proficiency are so bound, either by the dance "steps" and "patterns" they've been
taught or by traditional compositional methods, that they can no longer create
freely. Many of them show signs of a great deal of creative ability but have
become so afraid of criticism, or of not doing something "by the rules"—in
other words, afraid of being "wrong" (morality in art, again, creeping in in
a most damaging way)—that they never developed access into themselves for
their own individual and unique ways of perceiving the world. True, this need
for absolute direction and for being "right" often stems from more personal
causes, but freer creative methods might have helped these dancers to greater
confidence in themselves. For most of them it seems to be too late for real
creative freedom. A few take to more creative methods with relief, as to
something long sought; but most give up after a short time, because the re-
examination and relearning are difficult, and some never try at all. It is easier
to live with old habits, as with old, limiting emotional patterns. This loss of
individual creative potential is very sad; and it is important to realize how
and why it happens, because it is the current result of most of our dance teaching and could easily be the end result of all our proposed dance education in
schools unless we protect the creative life of our students beginning with the
time when they are very small and creating most freely. If dancers who are
now only performers, not artists, eventually teach, as many of them will, they
will again perpetuate the methods which harmed them; for most of them don't
even know that it has happened to them, though some feel regrets and long
to do what they are no longer free to do.

I'd like to say, at this point, that I've known many non-artist educators who
I felt did a beautiful job of teaching creatively and were well qualified to direct
a neophyte artist; and I've also known a lot of artists who couldn't teach at all.
I've known a lot of "educators" who didn't understand how to teach anything
creatively and certainly had no business teaching art; and I've had the great
privilege of knowing some artists who were fine teachers. There seems to be
no magic formula. As an older artist, though, I'd prefer being taught by an
artist, no matter how poor he may be as a teacher, because he has lived his
work, made his commitment to it, taken risks for it, and completely under-
stands its problems. There are some things a non-artist cannot give. But I
also believe that by concentrating on helping the pupil to be more open, and
with understanding of the work attitudes necessary for fresh art expression, a

creative educator can teach the young. The trouble is that there will be so few who can really do this well, and the rest will be doing a lot of harm. It isn't true in the field of art that "poor teaching is better than none."

I think the worst happens to the field of dance as a whole when, as in some of our colleges, dance educators teach educators who teach educators, and none of them ever spends enough time away from the protection and sponsorship of an institution to find out why an artist does things the way he does, or what he experiences from the world. A civil war develops, harmful to the art life of entire communities, to the schools, and to the independent artists. The perpetual circle of teachers tends to grow inward upon itself, feeding itself by supplying teachers for other positions in other schools, and forming its own "academy," depending upon the aesthetic views held by the group as a whole. Because schools are the most frequent source of dance sponsorship, these educators are in positions of considerable power, able to grant or withhold invitations to practicing artists, sometimes on very personal and tenuous grounds having little to do with artistic merit. Aside from national "name" artists and "safe," malleable student choreographers, they often find it difficult to recognize mature artists not developed under their hands, and can represent a source of considerable frustration and discouragement for the dance artist. Never having been without help, facilities, resources, and contacts, they have little understanding of what kind of support is necessary for the continued existence of an artist's work. This happens in all creative fields, though we hear more about it from writers because they have more opportunity to express themselves directly. When I am (as occasionally I have been) accused of "negativism" in my outlining of artists' problems and needs, the charge comes only from dance educators, never from artists in the field, who instead describe what I say as "courageous and positive."

Because many of these college dance educators will be teaching those who will teach dance on lower grade levels, this is extremely relevant. We can't allow ourselves to be so unsure of the ability of our students and so afraid of choices in our own thinking that we limit the creative vision of our students. Nor must we be so complacent and self-satisfied that we come armed with our lists and book references and think we know all about art, prepared to give all the answers. Some dance educators I have known have been dedicated helpers; some have been condescending judges, self-appointed. An artist must make friends with uncertainty; and to the extent that the educators really wish to help develop the artists that pass through their hands, they must help them feel comfortable with and even excited by the risks they might take for their own work, rather than urging them, always, to be "safe" in an institutional position. Some should take their chances and make their commitments to their work outside school positions.

As a partial remedy for this situation, which exists in almost all portions of our educational system already offering art education, I suggest that, for instance, those who are going to teach dance or any art at even a moderately advanced level should have some time set aside as a "non-resident term," during which the prospective teacher should apprentice himself actively to a professional artist in his field or during which he, himself, should try to do independent art work of his own. (Artists should also learn more about how to teach, but this is harder to arrange. The civil war can best be resolved by a sojourn of each, artist and teacher, in the land of the other.) Bennington College and Antioch already have a credited "non-resident term," so that students can gain practical experience in the field; and to judge from my own acquaintance with the practice, it seems mutually valuable and satisfactory. The artists, incidentally, usually welcome the help. I believe that only by living the life of an artist can one understand the interaction between artist and community. One cannot understand what one has not experienced. Often "I don't know" is the only beginning for learning, and certainly "I don't understand" paves the way for explanation and understanding.

There must be more interaction. Anyone who plans to teach any creative art on any level should spend some time learning from an artist "in the field," and not just from teachers of teachers. The colleges do serve a need by bringing major artists in for special classes. Perhaps more often on elementary levels, too, practicing artists can be brought in, either to be "in residence" (colleges have had such residents in graphic arts for some time, and are beginning to have them in dance) or for special classes. Any artist I can think of could give children a very memorable day, without benefit of a teaching credential.

But we do have some teachers of so-called "creative" dance who actually provide all subject matter, including stories (by no means necessary), for children's classes, and then even show the children exactly what movement should be done for the dances. Not all that is labeled "creative" is creative. This kind of dance teaching is equivalent to a "creative" painting class in which the teacher actually paints "a house" for the child. The children are quite capable of providing all subject matter and content for themselves, and will give a great deal more than we could think of, ourselves, if we just let them. All we have to do is lead them with questions. Teaching isn't a war, and children don't have to be made to learn. They really want to learn, if we can find ways to keep from stopping them. Maria Montessori was right about that much.

Dance teachers, like other teachers, sometimes try to get their students to do things which will reflect credit upon them, rather than things that are, strictly speaking, good for the students. Space does not allow presentation of a methodology here. I can only raise questions. Often, after I've spoken out on the problems of teaching dance creatively to adults and children, people say to me, "But you've said what *not* to do, and I wanted to know what to *do*." My point is exactly that the whole thing is much more simple and natural than we assume it is. Mature artists keep trying to reapproach the freedom they had as children, unhampered by the influences of their training.

The story goes that a child with obvious native talent was once brought to Matisse, and the parent asked, "How shall we train him further?"

Matisse answered, "Leave him alone and let him work by himself." Because the children know it all, and only need practice.

"But people probably won't leave him alone," Matisse added, regretfully. "Sooner or later they'll ruin him."

We are so busy rushing around and trying to keep children busy that they have no time to themselves to create. They need time to be themselves. With a simple introduction to the elements of the art, and with the implanted idea that creation in a medium is possible, they can often be left alone with the materials, the opportunity, and an atmosphere conducive to creative work. They also need time to sit down and reflect quietly upon what they are doing. A teacher must himself be aware enough of what it feels like to make something that he knows at what point his pupil is in the process of creating.

I trust the ability of the children, and I try to communicate this faith to them. I try to resist asking them to do things which I, as an artist, wouldn't want to do, such as being called away from their work when they are really concentrating on it. I need time to think, and so do they. I sometimes need encouragement, and so do they. I sometimes wish someone else would solve a problem for me, and so do they; but it is better for me if I do it myself, and it is also better for them. I respect them as artists.

I have taught at all levels in both public and private schools and universities, and recently had the opportunity, too, to teach creative dance classes of all elementary school levels, in a slum area, boys and girls together. Though I wasn't able to stay there longer than a day, and though I know from experience that as they came to know me better there would be a period of trial and adjustment, in the twenty minutes each class danced with me the children's faces were alight with the revelation of their own freedom. This was in marked contrast to folk dance classes I observed in the same school, where the children looked as if they felt they were in jail. There was no spontaneity to these classes, and they violated the idea of folk dancing completely in their grim and silly adherence to patterns holding no cultural or personal meaning for the children. When I left the building after the creative classes at the end of the day, about six burly little boys, from seven to twelve years old, vied with each other to see who would carry the teaching equipment to my car, and they ran after the car, waving, for as long as they could see me, begging me to return.

It can be done, but it must be done well. Unless we see far more change in current uncreative, stopgap teaching methods of arts now in our schools, I cannot advocate the addition of another art field to meet the same fate. I don't believe we will do what we really mean to do. I believe we will end by fostering mediocrity, by standardizing what should be free, and by crushing spontaneity. The chance to learn more about themselves and just to be themselves means a great deal to children; and, well-meaning though we may be, we give them but few opportunities.

# 18

# The Specialist's Role
# in Teaching

## by Betty Rowen

Many things have contributed to a heightened awareness of the need for the inclusion of dance in the curriculum of the elementary schools. A reaction against materialism and conformity has made us search for new values, has brought new recognition of the need for an aesthetic dimension to education. Ways to encourage creativity are being investigated, and dance cannot be neglected as a means to this end. Great interest in programs for the disadvantaged has called attention to areas of learning that had previously been overlooked. The development of perceptual motor skills as they relate to reading and language development gives further emphasis to the need for movement activity as part of the curriculum in the early grades.

Certainly now, more than ever, dance can make an important contribution to the total education of the young child. But who is prepared to teach dance in the elementary schools?

A survey of dance activity in 1961 revealed that "the ways in which dance has come into the public schools throughout the country are . . . extremely varied."[1] Sometimes it is a classroom teacher who has initiated dance activity. Sometimes it is a member of the physical education department, or a music teacher who uses dance as part of her program. No state has as yet established standards for certification of dance specialists. (There are specialists and distinct specialty areas for music, art, home economics. The dance teacher, however, must hold a license in some other field.) Generally, dance programs exist where the effect of a strong personality with a vital interest in dance has managed to innovate a program for a particular school or school system.

The situation today has not changed, although the needs for specialization

[1] Betty Rowen, "Terpsichore in the Classroom," *Dance Magazine,* October, 1961, p. 70.

in dance are greater. Dance as an art form has begun to be rightfully recognized in education, and departments are being established on college campuses under the jurisdiction of schools or departments of fine arts. Now dance majors do not receive an automatic license to teach physical education, as they may have done previously. By moving into the fine arts area, the dance major has lost her certificate to teach in the public schools.[2]

The certification of dance specialists by state departments of education is essential. A principal may very well want to hire a specialist to initiate a program of dance in his school, but the board of education is going to require the proper credentials. If the state does not provide such a license, the principal must find devious means to employ the dance specialist under some other type of contract, or must abandon the idea of a dance program altogether.

Is a specialist necessary?  A dance specialist is as necessary in the elementary school setting as is a specialist in music, art, or reading. Specialists in these areas serve as consultants supplying materials and ideas to classroom teachers. A reading specialist, for example, does not conduct the reading program for every grade of the elementary school. This would be an impossible task, and every classroom teacher must be properly prepared to teach in this area. The reading specialist has additional training, however, and is prepared not only to work with the classroom teacher to help her plan her program, but also to provide stimulation and advice to make the program more effective.

The dance specialist, too, should be a person with special training. She should have direct experience with dance as an art form either through study as a dance major on a college campus or through professional performance. She should also be qualified through courses in child development, pedagogy, and kinesiology to plan programs suitable for various age groups. She should be familiar with the teaching situation through some direct experience as student teacher, intern, or previous studio teacher.

Many capable teachers of dance do not meet academic requirements for teaching, and some allowance should be made to permit dancers with professional performance experience, and/or private dance teaching experience, to qualify for employment in public schools. Summer institutes or in-service training might be a way to prepare teachers with these kinds of experiences to function as dance specialists. Temporary licenses might be issued until requirements for certification are completed. Such arrangements have satisfied a need in other areas where there has been a shortage of qualified personnel. The professional artist has often had to sacrifice formal education in his youth, in order to pursue more intensively his professional goals. A performance career in dance is short-lived, and many performers who have passed the most

[2] Bruce King, "Dance in Our Schools: How Long Before the Issue Is Faced?" *Dance Magazine,* December, 1967, pp. 64-65.

productive age for work in the theater have many years left to devote to dance teaching. Educational institutions should be able to tap this rich source for potential teachers in the arts and to make suitable arrangements to put their talents to work in a school setting.

At the same time, adequate programs to train dance specialists must be carried on through study on college campuses. The dance major should have experience in performance, choreography, dance history and theory. But she should also have exposure to related modes of art as well as study in psychology, child development, and educational methods. She should have the opportunity to do student teaching, working under the supervision of a capable teacher of dance, even if such experience must be gained in private studios rather than the public elementary schools. (There simply are not enough good dance programs in the public schools to place all student teachers in them.) Some teaching experience with various age levels is essential, even if some of it must be gained through work in summer camps, recreational centers, and the like.

A college that sponsors such a program of dance education should receive accreditation for that program from the state department of education. In this way, any person successfully completing the program could qualify as a dance specialist in the public schools. In some states accreditation of a college program is not enough, and licenses must be issued based upon credentials submitted to the state department. In these cases, certification requirements must be established specifying credentials necessary for a license in dance, and applicants who meet these requirements can then apply directly to the state department. Until we have established accreditation of college dance programs or certification for dance specialists by state education departments as recognized and functioning policy, no fully effective dance program can be put into operation in the public elementary schools of this country.


Let us assume that we now have such a qualified dance specialist in an elementary school system. What is her role?

Her role would be basically that of a consultant. But to initiate the program, she would of course have to work intensively laying the groundwork. With the principals' and the superintendent's cooperation, she would offer orientation programs for the teachers. All teachers in the elementary schools of the district might be required to attend one such session, which might be held at a regularly scheduled faculty meeting. Teachers who are interested might then sign up for an in-service course in dance education conducted by the specialist. Increment credit should be offered for such a course, as it often is for a course in new methods of teaching mathematics or other subject areas.

In her first term in the school system, the dance specialist would arrange to give demonstration classes with each grade level in every elementary school. These classes would be carefully planned to meet the needs of particular age groups. They would be geared to the interests of the children and their physical capabilities, as well as oriented toward a relationship to an area of content of the curriculum for that grade. For example, a second-grade class studying simple machines in their science program might explore through movement the ways in which levers, pulleys, and screws operate. A sixth-grade class studying life in the Colonies might do work themes on building a log cabin, or might learn an Early American square dance. The teacher of the class might continue to work with the children on the project initiated by the dance specialist. Demonstrations of culminating projects might be shown to the entire school. The response of children to these demonstration lessons by the dance specialist, and to the demonstrations presented by other children, will do more to convince the teachers of the value of dance in the curriculum than any pressure brought to bear by the specialist or the administration. Children love to move, and a well-presented initial exposure to dance activity is bound to generate their enthusiasm.

Hopefully, every class in each elementary school of the district will ultimately include dance activity as part of its program. But the dance specialist, after this initial introductory period, would simply be available for consultation. She cannot be expected to teach all of the dance that should take place in the elementary school setting. The classroom teacher, who knows the children and the curriculum, is in a much better position to introduce movement exploration at whatever time seems desirable. To wait two or three weeks at a time for the dance specialist to visit the classroom would defeat the essential purpose of the program. Dance should be part of the daily activity of children in the elementary grades. For too long teachers have relied on verbal, didactic, and sedentary forms of communication and have neglected the motivational power of movement in learning.

Having initiated a program in dance, the specialist would not operate on a set weekly or monthly program. Her visits to the classroom would be made upon invitation from the classroom teacher. When a new project was being introduced, the classroom teacher would discuss it with the specialist, who might then visit the class to help with its initial presentation. As a dance activity idea approaches culmination, the specialist might again be invited to help the children with their choreography. Each week the specialist would make up her schedule based on the teachers' requests which had been submitted to her on a designated day of the previous week. This type of program for the specialist has proved most effective in school systems where art and music are functional and important parts of the curriculum.[3]

In performing this role, the specialist's specific functions include the following responsibilities:

---

[3] The Ridgewood, N. J., school system reported on this method at the NJEA Convention in Atlantic City, November, 1966.

1. She would work with teachers, giving workshops and in-service courses on the use of movement in the classroom.
2. She would give demonstration classes, visiting in the classroom and initiating a movement program the teacher would then pursue on her own.
3. She would help the classroom teacher to plan movement experiences related to the curriculum for a particular class.
4. She would supply records, rhythm instruments, and resource materials on request by teachers.
5. She would plan assembly programs to give children the opportunity to perform dances they had created or learned.
6. She would conduct a dance club for children interested in more intensive study.
7. She would invite guest artists to the schools, and would prepare introductory materials to present to children before scheduled performances.

If the classroom teacher is to carry out the program in dance for her class, how is she to be prepared for this role? The teacher need not be a dancer, but some movement experience should be part of her college training. A dance course which allows for creative expression at the student's own level should be a significant part of the preparation of every prospective teacher of young children. The teacher must experience the creative process personally in order to know how to induce it in children. The aliveness and neuromuscular sensitivity which are the products of a challenging dance experience will provide ready identification with the movement responses of children. Only through participation will the teacher understand the prominent role that dance can play in the total development of the child.

Teacher preparation programs on college campuses must take into account the need for creative experiences for all who plan to work with children. A minor in one area of the arts, whether music, drama, dance, or graphic art, would be an advisable requirement for prospective elementary school teachers. The sense of involvement that we hope to be able to induce in children must be experienced by the teacher herself, if we hope to develop creative and aesthetically aware individuals in our schools.

Of course, the child has a head start in this area. All young children, to a greater or lesser degree, come into school with a receptivity to sensory experience and an enjoyment of movement. If, through dance activity, we can keep alive this responsiveness and aesthetic sensitivity, we can make the elementary school program one that prepares individuals for a richer and more meaningful life.

# 19

## Dance and the Classroom Teacher

### by Ruth D. Dillard

As principal of an elementary school, I try to be aware of the effect that my attitudes, philosophy, and perspective have upon the school staff and, hence, upon the instructional program. When confronted with a question concerning the desirability and importance of dance in the school curriculum, I had to examine my philosophy of early childhood education.

Education for young children is not a preparation for living—it *is* living. It must be real, dynamic, relevant to the individual; it must be sufficiently abrasive to whet the intellectual appetite for "more": continued and extended experiencing, planning, exploring, evaluating, probing, and experimenting. Since education is living, it cannot be acquired without involvement of mind, body, and emotions. The educative process appears to develop best in a responsive environment, where youngsters are accepted as they are, where activities are based on a knowledge of child development, an understanding of the learning process, and clear perception of our goals for children.

We base our planning for young children on these principles, whether we are planning an entire curriculum, a day's program, or a single learning experience. What, then, should we include? How should we plan?

Let's *not* make school a bore, a tedium of monotony, days of lows with no highs, lacking in balance between freedom and guidance, sedentary and physical activity, group and individual pursuits. Let's *not* restrict education to "learning to read," "reading to learn," computation, and the other academic subjects. We know this point of view collapsed with the Stutz "Bearcat."

A rich curriculum is merely a plan for a full, multifaceted life for children at school. It includes those experiences which sensitize the child to beauty—to sights, smells, sounds, movements, and feelings. It provides opportunities for emotional release as well as emotional control, the chance to create as well as the necessity for self-discipline. Dance meets these criteria.

Is dance, then, a desirable and necessary activity to be included in the curriculum for young children? Of course! Can healthy youngsters *live* without running, sliding, skipping, hopping, leaping, weaving, twisting, or turning? No? Then, the child *must* dance in school!

One of the basic laws of teaching is to utilize whatever the child brings to school. He brings his body, full of energy and zing, capable of gathering all sorts of impressions through the senses, and capable of expressing these impressions through motion. Dance provides the opportunity for conscious exploration of time, space, and force. It develops clear concepts of high and low, slow and fast, softness and great effort. Dance promotes creativity, for each child's dance is his own. It is a new accomplishment which brings a greater sense of adequacy, a deeper sense of selfhood than before. Dance contributes to mastery of the body, to its control and coordination; both are important keys to pride as well as to health.

If dance is an integral part of a rich curriculum, who is to teach it? Artists may assume the stance that the art of the dance will surely be diluted and degraded unless it is handled by the expert. I have even been told that the dancer alone is sufficiently knowledgeable about the muscular maturation of youngsters to insure instruction without injury. Somehow, I find this difficult to believe.

At any rate, are the experts available? How many public school systems employ dance instructors on a regular basis? Are our children to be denied the joys and benefits of dance while we await the social, economic, and cultural upheaval necessary to the provision of skilled dancers as full-time instructors in elementary schools?

If our children have survived the trite, overdone "rhythms" which have been ladled out to them throughout the years, surely they would benefit from a dance program which is dynamic and well sequenced. There are books—by Ruth Murray, Emma Sheehy, and others—that can serve quite adequately as guides for the classroom teacher.

Who is in a better position to teach dance on the elementary level than the classroom teacher? I defend her as the most knowledgeable person concerning the physical, emotional, and social needs of her children. She can best utilize daily observation to diagnose the children's needs based on their current level of motor development, movement experiences, daily living, and personal interests. She knows best that Billy is having difficulty with his "sets," talks very little because of a stutter, cannot run as fast as the other boys, but creates exciting dancelike movements for his partner to "mirror."

The classroom teacher can plan activities for the most appropriate part of the day, instead of being forced to "motivate" dance at an inconvenient time because of the difficulties of scheduling. This would present a problem, were we to depend upon the artist. So many opportunities occur during the day when dance would provide the perfect change of pace or the perfect opportunity for a specific teaching point that would be missed by the specialist.

If Susan brought beautiful feathers to school, what a marvelous opportunity for exploring, discovering, demonstrating, and communicating. The thrill may be gone, and certainly the timeliness, should we wait for the specialist's scheduled visit. The children would want to respond to and explore the many things that can be done with feathers, today!

Teaching is not made of discrete units; we believe in reinforcement through interrelated activities. The classroom teacher is fully aware of the experiences and activities provided throughout the day in developing all aspects of the curriculum. This knowledge would facilitate the planning for a balanced dance program including some technique, rhythms, improvisation, and composition. It would also facilitate a well-balanced instructional program resulting from the effective timing of a variety of activities. Check lists, diaries, posters, and tambourines could all be parts of a well-correlated and interrelated program. The classroom teacher can intensify the relatedness of music, art, dance, and dramatic play. She can take time to explore an activity fully, because her schedule is flexible. The teacher can utilize a functional spiral approach to dance instruction which could be effective since she is with the class every day.


Can the classroom teacher teach dance? My question is: "Who else?"

# VII

## *Evaluation in the Arts*

Most researchers have avoided trying to deal with the problem of evaluation in the arts. Part of this problem is that evaluation in education is presently conceived of as a standardized paper-and-pencil test which measures a minor skill or an assumed characteristic. Such tests are usually inappropriate for the arts. Martha Rashid proposes adapting (to the school situation) assessment items which have already been developed within the tradition of the arts, in the form of art criticism. She discusses the use of the controversial behavioral objectives and the traditional misuse of evaluative tools. Dr. Rashid's article suggests a compromise between the artist and the behaviorist that would provide the educator with a systematic way of improving educational programs for young children through the proper use of effective evaluation.

Chapter 21 is a specific example of an alternative to "all or nothing." Dance cannot be fragmented. Its aesthetic qualities demand a wholistic way of approaching both its expression and its evaluation. We have identified *some* observable behaviors that can be evaluated by *dancers* and trained educators. These items do not represent dance. They are only pieces of something much greater than the items themselves, but they represent *some* desirable aims of dance, and they allow evaluation of programs.

# 20

# Metrics and the Muses

## by Martha Rashid

Metrics and the muses? The ultimate in polarities! Metrics is exact, quantitative, elegantly precise. The muses, on the other hand, defy precision and quantification. So goes the traditional antiphony leading to what has become a seemingly natural antipathy between those who attempt to quantify and those who attempt to express, to create, and to interpret. Because the objectives and processes of measurement seem to be as different from the objectives and processes characteristic of the arts as it is possible for one human activity to be from another, there has been an understandable reluctance to link the two in any serious discussion of the place of the arts in the education of children.

Such reluctance has not, however, characterized the arts in general. Art criticism has served as a form of sustained assessment of the nature and role of the arts in human society. The emergence of the critic probably followed very closely on that of the composer and the performer, in some special dawning of human prehistory. But speculation about the genesis of art criticism is not our purpose here. Whenever and however criticism may have begun, the task of the critic seems to have been to examine, to describe, and to explain the qualities of a general or particular art form. (Or to "explain away" these qualities, as one may be tempted to say in the case of some critics.) In pursuing the general goal of describing and explaining, criticism has also undertaken to relate an art form to an artistic tradition and to a social context and thus to discourse upon its relevance to the lives of whatever "audience" the art form has reached beyond the time and place of those who had the benefit of immediate experience. It is possible to discern among the purposes of art criticism a basic function of measurement or assessment, although such criticism admittedly seems very different from the points, scores, and percentile rankings we typically associate with school testing programs.

The purpose of this chapter is to examine some of the broad issues involved in developing adequate means of evaluating the arts as they are usually included in school programs for young children. (And to say "usually" is to realize that the arts receive short shrift in many school programs—because of pressures for including "useful" offerings and also for other reasons discussed elsewhere in this volume.) Thus we move from the function of criticism in the arts to a different, systematic form of assessment appropriate to a particular institutional setting.

Evaluation of a curricular offering can take protean forms and can be accomplished on many different levels. The complex task of evaluating the arts begins with placing them in an appropriate framework of objectives or goals. The task of identifying long-range and daily instructional objectives, whose achievement is to be measured in some way, cannot be separated from that of identifying and selecting the indicators of such curricular objectives. The term "indicators" is used because an important canon of evaluation is that children's behavior is only sampled, not exhaustively catalogued. Evaluation items or situations, therefore, presumably should be the best possible indicators of a child's performance in the domain of behavior being sampled over a given period of time. Heretofore, the selection and use of specified indicators has been considered the sole province of experts in measurement. Such a viewpoint is disastrous! The usual practice of shaping a curriculum and then administering a battery of tests at an end point of the instructional sequence does at least two damaging things. It separates the process of curriculum developmen from the process of evaluation. It provides a narrow view of evaluation as only a measurement of some product or other. The product traditionally has been factual knowledge. Although long-range objectives may have been broadly formulated to go beyond convergent bits and pieces of knowledge, in actual practice evaluation has become synonymous with testing situations where facts can be easily recalled and written down to fit a prescribed test format. Such easy-recall testing has been only too characteristic of evaluation in the language arts, mathematics, science, and the social studies. For the most part, evaluation in the arts has been on a catch-as-catch-can basis.

The state-of-the-art of this phase of evaluation is explored further in another section of this chapter. The point to be made now is that those who are responsible for evaluation must plan in tandem with those who are responsible for setting goals and developing instructional materials. Otherwise we will continue to present children with a truncated program—a program with a broad chasm between stated objectives and the indicators used to determine whether the objectives have been realized. We may, for example, eagerly endorse the need for young children to explore, to extend, and to use the vocabulary of movement. And if we limit evaluation only to measuring children's understanding of dance terms on a vocabulary test, then we use evaluation to countermand, rather than to measure the achievement of, our stated goals.

Recently there has been quite a stir in educational circles over the form to use in stating instructional objectives. What will the child be doing which is observable? In what situation will he be exhibiting such behavior? What is the minimum level of acceptable performance? Answers to questions such as these are an important part of the technology for stating instructional objectives in behavioral terms. As is usual in education, the protagonists and antagonists of behavioral objectives have manned their respective battle stations. Protagonists hail behavioral objectives as an effective way out of the abysmal morass of introspection in curriculum development. When teachers plan instruction only in terms of observable behavior occurring in situations that can be objectively described, the protagonists argue, then teachers can also stipulate clearly the indicator or measurement item that can be used to sample the occurrence of the behavior described in the objective. Antagonists decry the emphasis on behavioral objectives as the latest dehumanizing force in an educational conspiracy, and their criticism ebbs and flows over the philosophical shoals of a primitive Watsonian form of behavioristic psychology. What has all this to do with children, the arts, the schools? Does the form of a statement of objectives actually have anything to do with "real life" in classrooms? Does it mean that music or dance may be taught differently? Does it mean that children may be presented with opportunities for different experiences?

Because the present professional controversy over the statement of objectives is important, and because it is more complex historically and philosophically than the opening comments above may have indicated, it is necessary to be selective and to discuss only those aspects of the situation which relate in some way to evaluation. One important consequent of using behavioral objectives is that emphasis has shifted from the nobility of phrasing in ultimate objectives to the homely phrasing of what it is that children and teachers actually do in classrooms day by day. Such a shift does not mean that we have disavowed general ultimate objectives. It is only that it is difficult if not impossible for a teacher directly, once and for all, to teach, for example, "aesthetic sensibility." It is not particularly difficult for a teacher to approach the component parts of "aesthetic sensibility" and to arrange for many different experiences, over a period of time, in which children interact with color, line, texture, and form. There is a practical concern here in respect to manageability. How do we expect the teacher to manage the instructional situation in the classroom? When the ultimate objective is rephrased in the terminology of specific instructional situations, it does become more manageable for the teacher because it is more comprehensible. How does this affect evaluation? In brief, evaluation may become a daily sampling of the learning process and not an end-product measurement. The emphasis has shifted from what may be laudable but unmeasurable ultimate objectives to workable and measurable objectives. Teachers, children, and evaluation experts can talk more intelligently and objectively about observable samples of behavior. This is not to say that the more vaguely worded long-range objectives are unimportant. It is only to say: "Let's spend most of our time and effort on improving behaviors which are manageable, observable, and measurable."

Much of the controversy over behavioral objectives has to do with the feasibility of measuring what it is we purport to teach. Admittedly there have been abuses and misuses of tests at all educational levels. When the functions of measurement are not understood, when evaluation is limited to test scores and kept separate from the daily instructional process, misuse and abuse follow. The historical fact of mismanagement of evaluation should not, however, be used as an argument against the feasibility of measuring what we aim to teach. Much better arguments can be used. The complex interaction of clusters of variables which affect the learning process, the cumulative nature of learning, the weak and often unwieldly theoretical systems underlying the constructs we use—these are much more telling arguments against the feasibility of measuring what we aim to teach and what children actually learn. As for the argument that much of what we teach is, by nature, immune to measurement, one can only agree and proceed to work on those areas of human development which are either observable or lend themselves to some form of comprehensibility for inclusion in a curricular design.

However instructional objectives are defined and derived for use in a framework for curriculum and evaluation, a basic issue facing curriculum experts (in this case read "teachers") is the degree of emphasis to place on roles or varying functions within the arts. How much emphasis, for example, should be placed on the role of the performer? Should the role of critic or historian be considered in programs for young children? Should young childen be expected to compose or choreograph? All of these questions affect evaluation via the effects their resolution has upon actual instructional programs. It is difficult to see how any of these roles can be *kept out* of a school program which has any vitality or verisimilitude relative to the arts as they are outside the school environs. It is only the most unimaginative and drearily pedantic program which can hold children back from composing, from performing, from reflecting upon the qualities of their own or someone else's work. It is only the restrictive program issuing from reams of mimeographed patterns and exercises which keeps children from practicing all the roles and specialties in the arts as they actually identify the structure and heuristics inherent in those aspects of the arts they experience.

In respect to an evaluation of the effectiveness of any role as perceived and carried out by children, we must begin with expectations of childlike behavior. We cannot expect mature playing of roles; but at each general development level, in each individual situation, we adjust our interpretation of the indicators of role competence to factors such as previous experience, acuity of perception, sex role adequacy, strength of ego system, and emerging preference for one role over another. Here again, evaluation is directed to process and not merely to product. Indicators or evaluation items must be framed and used in accordance with the hard-won principles that determine the development of human beings. Evaluation of children's role competence in the arts must be viewed against the backdrop of what is known about child development. Does the child perceive that fluidity of movement is essential to interpreting a particular emotional situation? Can he demonstrate or identify a relatively more fluid movement? Shall we expect him to explain on the verbal level, or by movement alone? Does he "feel" the fluidity in the very marrow of his bones? Does he think it's "sissy" to demonstrate, to identify, or to discuss fluidity of movement? These questions may not be pertinent to the framing of particular indicators or measurement items in respect to role competence. They are very pertinent, however, to how the teacher interprets and uses the information derived from measurement situations. Performance on a measurement item does not explain a child's behavior; it is, rather, an objective description. Thus the most important part of the evaluation process begins with the teacher's interpretation of the objectively described behavior sample. It is at this point that questions such as those above must be entertained by the teacher and, at times, by teacher and child thinking together.

"Beauty is eternity gazing at itself in a mirror." Intimations of the essence of beauty are as numerous as definitions of art. Kahlil Gibran's conception of beauty does suggest to those of us who work with children that the wellsprings of artistic impulse and achievement come from within, whether we think of individual or collective human history. This view is not antithetical to that which makes behavior a touchstone of evaluation. Given the behavior the teacher observes, she can use all she knows about each child, while also (perhaps more important) leading him to look inward, to help him express the beauty that is his. This constant interchange between the inner being and the real world of color, melody, texture, and pattern is the (often silent) dialogue which must be encouraged and not squashed by what we adults signify as important in school programs. When the curriculum is not ordered in such a way that it communicates to children what adults really consider important, then very often the trivial, the routine, the easily recallable will be what is perceived by children and accepted by them as important. Unfortunately, such perceptions too often are valid. It is sad that we do not leave room and time for the really important processes of human development in the ever expanding elementary school curriculum. It is even sadder that we permit children to feel that reflection, meditation, and "the silent dialogue" are among the least-honored processes in the classroom. Time to think and time to create must not be shoved out of the curriculum by pressures engendered by the knowledge explosion and the expectations of the public that schools can be used to cure all social ills. Diatribe? Perhaps. But what is not included in the curriculum can-not be evaluated. And so often what cannot easily be measured is not includ-ed. So the circumference of the circle can be as exclusive as it can be inclusive.

How then can we evaluate or measure in the arts the processes which seem so basic to the arts? Are reflection, selectivity, and creativity amenable to measurement? Can such elusive human activities be scaled and quantified? At present the answer is negative. But there is no inherent difficulty. We have scaled intelligence and derived reasonably practical indicators and predictors of intelligent behavior. The best items on an intelligence test are instructive because they do sample what is generally considered to be intelligent behavior. Comparisons with similar groups derive norms which are the basis for judge-ments used to peg such behaviors at a particular level. Why cannot similar procedures be developed in the arts? Current tests of creativity do leave much to be desired. They provide, however, some useful do's and don't's for enlarg-ing our efforts and applying them to many different aspects of development and learning in the arts. If we continue to emphasize only the intangibility of the arts and their imperviousness to measurement of any kind, *in school situations for children,* then we are refusing to acknowledge the rich heritage of art criticism. Let us go to the canons of assessment which have been developed within the traditions of the arts themselves in the form of criticism. These must then be identified, selected, and modified in respect both to curriculum objectives and to the characteristics of children. Evaluation cannot be adjunc-tive to education in the arts. It must be an integral part of the arts program if we wish to achieve a systematic way to keep improving instructional pro-grams.

# 21

# Assessing Progress toward Creativity: A Proposal

## by Martin Haberman and Tobie Meisel

Creative expression has a context, a form, a medium; it takes shape with particular materials and utilizes a distinctive mode of communication. Is a person who is creative in one area also creative in others? This sounds like a better question than it is, since there is no adequate way to evaluate creative expression apart from its particular form.

The attempt to delimit a general ability which can be labeled "creativity" leads to naive tests which not only build assumption upon assumption but also confuse operational definitions with reality. How *many* uses can you think of for a newspaper? How *fast* can you do it? How *unusual* are the responses? ("Cut it up for a kidnap note": maybe one in ten thousand?) Supposedly, test items such as these get at something someone labels "divergence," which can be taught by a method someone else calls "brainstorming," which will lead to a generalizable quality a third expert calls "creativity." Nonsense!

The question of the degree to which creativity is a general rather than a specialized ability is a false one. Creative expression is demonstrated utilizing a particular subject matter or art form; its assessment should be in the context of these distinctive manifestations.

Our assumptions about creativity are these: that it is a process of making applications of knowledge; that it involves objective manifestations as well as internal states of being; that it is the result of learning skills and techniques but cumulates to more than the sum of these discrete parts; that it can be learned but not directly taught; that it can be evaluated by teachers and pupils as well as by experts; and that it is cultivated and expressed in some particular form (dance, for example) rather than in general.

A problem, three types of approach to its solution, and a proposal are discussed here, based on the example of dance. While some of the evaluative criteria offered use words that seem to correspond with language used in other disciplines, all the criteria derive from definitions based on the dance vocabulary and not on the belief in a singular, global creative capacity.

## THE PROBLEM

Dance is an art form. It communicates more than the tangible. But the skills of dance are, by definition, behavioral. It is even possible to subdivide these skills into movement activities which can be learned by very young children. Lessons for five-year-olds, for example, might involve walking and other basic locomotor movements, moving on different levels, moving in various directions on alternate paths, and combinations of these and other movements. But the questions that remain to be answered are: Where do such demonstrated behaviors lead? How can we recognize long-term achievement as well as immediate progress?

## APPROACHES TO SOLUTIONS

1. The *behavioral approach* suggests dealing only with observable achievements. Although recognizing that learning to dance will take the student way beyond the demonstrable, this approach still maintains that a sizable and basic part of dance is behavioral and can be broken into subparts, and that these subparts will add up to a good share of what dancers do. Admitting that some or even much of dance is beyond present measurement and assessment techniques, this approach emphasizes confining what schools try to teach and evaluate to discernible behaviors. The behaviorist asks: "How can that which is undiscernible and beyond evaluation possibly be taught or assessed?"

2. The *aesthetic approach* emphasizes that the bits and pieces of skills and technique do not add up to, and may even interfere with, understanding of basic concepts—concepts which are beyond evaluation. This group includes artists who harbor a strong doubt that creative expression in one person can be taught or even nurtured by another. The solution they offer is: "Never lose sight of the whole. Each lesson, skill, or activity must be seen in context and in relation to some ultimate forms."

The dancer believes in building his art on a firm mastery of technique. On this level he is in tune with the behaviorist. However, the dance artist would question equating or even relating the movement of young children to the mature expression of the art form. He would also insist that the sophisticated performance, while behavioral, is only possible by dancers utilizing the language of dance—and this is his fundamental difference with the behaviorist. The dancer questions the validity of trying to make his art general education. He doubts that the bits and pieces of any curriculum will add up to any basic concepts. For him, dance is infinitely more than the cumulation of behavioral skills. If pushed, he insists on waiting for the whole end product: "How can you really evaluate any training without waiting for a total, mature performance?"

3. The *middle ground* approach assumes that movement skills lead to dance and that since a part of dance is behavioral, it is partially accessible to general knowledge and evaluation. The middle ground is not a happy position, since it implies a lack of clarity and commitment. Nevertheless it seems most sensible to us, since it recognizes the obvious basis of art in mastery of techniques which can be evaluated in behavioral terms. This position assumes that movement is ultimately related to dance and that dance movement can and should be viewed as general education. We ask: "Admitting that the art form communicates more than can presently be assessed, why not evaluate wherever possible those behaviors which constitute a basic portion of the dancer's art?"

## A PROPOSAL

Utilize behaviorists to evaluate specific lessons cast in behavioral terms. (Does the child move on three levels or doesn't he? Can he skip or can't he? Will he remember a path he took to his friend or won't he?) Assume a relationship between this skill of movement and the potential for ultimately dancing. At the completion of an instructional program in dance, ask dancers rather than behaviorists to make over-all judgements on what all these skills add up to. The dance expert would view pupils' movement activity and then judge their individual progress in terms of criteria such as those we propose here. Two things must be remembered about these criteria. They refer to observable behaviors which are part of, but *not in themselves,* dance. The purpose of applying such criteria to individual student activity is not to assign grades or the like but to assess the quality of the instructional program with a view to revising it accordingly.

*For this purpose, then, assess the degree to which a student can:*

Move in a personal and expressive way.
Demonstrate a great many responses, initiating a wide variety of alternatives.
Demonstrate imaginative alternative(s) that solve a given problem.
Demonstrate persistence until reasonable success has been achieved.
Demonstrate physical and mental attention span appropriate to activity and age.
Demonstrate a cumulative effect of activity, recalling and using what was done previously.
Demonstrate ability to translate known concepts from other media into movement.
Demonstrate ability to translate known movement concepts into other media.
Demonstrate ability to pick up new movement ideas quickly and extend them readily.

Imitate partner's movements, quickly changing and copying his exact movements.

Continue demonstrating his interpretation after seeing different interpretations.

Demonstrate control and coordination in using his body.

Demonstrate increasing ability to lengthen response.

Demonstrate increasing ability to respond making fuller use of the body.

Demonstrate increasing ability to utilize and manipulate elements of space (range, direction, level, path).

Demonstrate increasing ability to utilize and manipulate the elements of time (tempo, pulse, rhythm, pattern, accent).

Demonstrate increasing ability to utilize the elements of force (sustained, percussive, relaxed, tense).

Demonstrate ability to observe and evaluate his own movements and movements of others.

Demonstrate the ability to compose a simple dance study.

Clearly, this proposal represents a middle position in which we attempt to utilize both the behaviorist's stress on the demonstrable and the artist's emphasis on wholeness. While the debate between the scientist and the aesthete has been exciting and interesting, perhaps it has gone on long enough. Those responsible for planning school programs must now decide to utilize both forms of specialization in instructional units that add up to a fundamental part of the final product.

# VIII

## The Child:
## Artist and Audience

Educators wonder what a dance program in the schools will lead to. Dancers themselves reflect on the meaning of the dance experiences in which they engage with young children.

Ann Halprin discusses the child's creative ability and the manner in which it should be shaped. Only if the child is allowed to be involved in society's moments of joy and tragedy, in the human metamorphosis, will he have the resources to become a true creator. In this view, dance is a communal experience of artist and audience.

Erika Thimey is concerned with communication and the performer's ability to elicit responses from an audience. Discussing the child's role as performer, she deals with the differences, in respect to production and choreography, between children's and adults' performing dance theater. When does the child become an effective performer, and what sort of audience is he for an adult professional dance group as opposed to a children's dance group? Does dancing for others, as distinguished from dancing for oneself, add new dimensions to a child's dancing?

Evelyn de la Tour looks along the artistic continuum containing both child and adult. She is concerned with criteria for judging performance and with the standards applied to these criteria in the case of the child and of the adult performer. More than this, she focuses directly on the question: "To what does it all lead?" She clearly explains the value of dance as general education for all, and then emphasizes that a good dance program should lead the interested and talented child to a career as a professional performer and choreographer.

# 22

## The Child Creating

### by Ann Halprin

Children's dance is avant-garde; as a creative activity it is in the best current direction of the new life style, the creative community. Dance is the creative community, representing the sum total of what a person is now: the capacity to feel, think, react, and express his feelings through movement and other sensory communication. We must forget some of our preoccupation with preparing for the future and start appreciating the *now*. Life is now, and now is the time for life and art to merge.

The Reverend Dr. Martin Luther King, Jr., was assassinated April 9 at 6:00 P.M. His funeral was on television for the whole world to attend. I watched his funeral, and, like many others, wept and struggled with my emotions. A momentous ritual was taking place, and deep and lasting Myth was being created; one of the great ceremonials of all modern times was being enacted. I watched the memorial films shown in connection with the funeral, and heard the great prophet's voice boom out, "Tell them I tried to love somebody . . ." Was there a soul listening and watching who was not shaken to his roots, and cleansed? I saw his four children, shaken and holding back tears like all the adults who were in the church—the dignitaries and the common folk. We saw his children, feeling with the same depth as everyone else, but where were *our* children? As closely as I watched, I saw no other children, in the church or marching. The children in the home where I watched TV were in their rooms all during the services, playing and laughing, completely unaware of this historical moment. They were not asked to come and watch. They were left separated from the adults.

Where were the children? Is this not their country and their history? We adults must realize that children are a part of humanity in its highest moments, tragic or joyous. Children understand, and feel as strongly as we. They do not need to be protected from emotional experience; when we "protect" them we

155

deny children their birthright: the right to feel deeply and express these feelings, to ask questions, to take responsibility, to be a living part of our society.

Our society regards children as "separate and equal" or "separate and better." Child-oriented activities deny that children have the same expressive
resources as adults, and the same expressive potential. And in our computerized,
rational, spectator-sport society, adults do not understand young people who
live straightforwardly and sensually. Adults, so long denied freedom in sensory
awareness and opportunity to experience fully the expressive aspects of movement, cannot identify with the experiences of young people. The adult is constantly asking the child to rationalize and justify in words that which is non-
verbal and experiential in value. The result is that our children are not integrated into society, that they have built their own society which recognizes no
total responsibility. But it is a society which takes seriously its feelings and
the expression of feelings in individual and community rites. Everywhere the
young people know they need and want *something* and are violently demonstrating that felt need for change. Everywhere young people are coming together in tribal gatherings where they mourn, celebrate, sing, and dance together. Everywhere dance is an expression of the new life style. Young people want to be free to be themselves, to interrelate, to celebrate *together* with
others the mysteries, the joys, and the sorrows of life and nature.

Parents must cope with what they do not understand, by accepting all of the
child's emotions and the ways he expresses them through any sensory medium
—painting, words, sound, or movement. This means avoiding censorship of
what the child feels or the forms the expressions of his feelings take.

The function of the dance teacher is complex. First, he helps the child
open the doors of self-awareness; second, he tries to foster awareness of other
individuals; third, he helps form a sense of community through dance. The
teacher is the catalyst opening up emotional states through the use of movement. Movement and feeling interact, feeding into each other; this feedback
process enables the child to become aware of how he as an individual can get
in touch with his own resources. Through increased awareness, the individual
recognizes how his movement affects other people, and how other people
affect him; he learns to dance with them. Teachers foster the third stage of
development, community involvement, by providing a setting in which the
individual and person-to-person dance experience can extend to a group experience with cultural significance. Through good teaching, the freedom to be
ourselves extends to the freedom to interrelate with others. This is the creative
community.

Samples of creative writing done after a dance lesson indicate that children
are enough aware of their feelings to express them both through movement
and in words. Children's dance says: "I am . . . I am my dance . . . I am my
experience." Children's words say:

I am full of tender touching, fragile, peaceful happiness.
My spiral dewdrops are growing.

RANA, age 13

I feel lonely, tired, distressed, like I'm in another world (space).
I'm quiet. I feel strange, afraid, I'm cold, alone. I'm absolutely
friendless.

ERICA, age 12

Here is an example of how children come to an expression of themselves.
The children fantasized that they were stones and rocks. Afterwards they
were given fistfuls of clay, and each made a clay model of the rock or stone
he was. When they were finished they placed their clay sculptures in the center of the circle into which we had gathered and told us what they saw. They
told us this way: "I am my sculpture. I am closed on the outside, but open
inside. I have long arms that are strong and can carry a lot." In order to help
children find their self-identity, and promote their self-awareness, the teacher
must say, "This is what you did. It is good. I like it." They also need the
group to share their experiences in words, feelings, and movement.

We are on the threshold of a reaffirmation of creativity as a community
force. There is a crying need for real community movement experience. Let
me quote a letter, one of dozens I received as a result of week-end seminars
at various colleges.

> In early March you came to Pomona College. Although I missed you, my
> friends did not. From their snapshots and enthusiastic descriptions I have
> grown interested. Alas, they're only able to recall a few of the exercises you
> brought. What I would like to do is put together a notebook of these (what
> do you call them?). Also I would like to know the philosophy behind them
> so that we can experiment and develop our own. I would appreciate it if you
> could tell me where to look to find more about these exercises in moving and
> feeling.

The what-do-you-call-thems referred to in the letter are experiences I call
"Myths," which evolved when our dance group, instead of performing for an
audience, decided to include the audience as participants. The Myths resulted
from my desire to evolve a setting for the spontaneous release of feelings and
movements through which could be developed the re-enactment of archetypal
community rites. The hope was that the Myth form and method could provide
the groundwork for self-initiated group dance rites to include people of all
ages, regardless of any formal training. These events have taken place in various "now" situations—on a grassy mall at Pomona, in a lounge at San Francisco
State, in a music building—usually not in a gymnasium or other usual locale
of "dance."

The format is kept deliberately simple to allow for maximum individual and group interplay. The Myth is experienced in a three-phase development. First, individuals find their own patterns. Then they use the expressive energy of these patterns to interact with one another in the environment. This inevitably leads to a spontaneous group ritual. The movement materials are carefully selected for the environment, light and sound carefully used, establishing an aesthetic context.

Here is how one very simple Myth, in which both children and adults participated, took form.

A group of fifty persons, some of them children, was divided into two groups. One (the "guest" group) was sent to a separate room and the other (the "host" group) was given the following instructions: alter the environment of your room for the guest group. The host group was provided materials such as boxes, sheets of plastic, risers, a scaffold, lights, large pieces of cloth and cardboard with which to build. A time limit of fifteen minutes was set for construction.

The result was a walk-through environment in which one group first built tunnels, bridges, caves, and other structures and then, acting as hosts, played various roles with the guest group. It was a sort of community in which people had definite roles and which was full of games and surprises.

After the guests had experienced for a while the environment built for them, they in turn were invited to build a new environment for the original host group, using the same materials and the same room. This became a much more difficult and more exciting task, for it involved destruction of the old structure as well as construction of a new and different one. The second building took longer and took a more simple and direct form. The excitement of destruction and rebuilding became a ritual of death and rebirth, a universal religious and mythological theme.

Kerenyi summarizes exactly our experience at that event when he says, speaking of the legend of Demeter and the Eleusinian mysteries (rites) connected with her and with the death and rebirth of Persephone:

> ... the knowledge that man must die but lives on in his descendants [or here in his works] is trivial. This is certainly true of mere knowledge of something. But there is a vast difference between *knowing* of something, *knowing it* and *being it*. It is one thing to *know* 'the seed and the sprout' and quite another to have recognized in them the past and future as one's *own being* and its continuum. ... A knowledge with this content, with the experience of being in death is not to be despised.[1]

[1] C. G. Jung & K. Kerenyi, *Essays on the Science of Mythology* (New York: Bollingen Foundation [Pantheon Books], 1949), p. 254.

This is the individual and also the group experience. Jung says that through sharing in ceremonial rites the individual symbolically lives through the experience of isolation (darkness, destructon, underworld) and is restored to wholeness. "All ritual preoccupation with archetypes ultimately has this aim and this result."

Our rebuilding did have this result, for the form of the building and the dance of entry was progressively simplified until it very closely resembled a primordial ritual of birth, ordeal, sacrifice, and finally triumph of life and vitality over all. The door to the room was blocked by a platform so that each entrant had to be pulled through the opening. Each entrant was then passed overhead from hand to hand by a line of men and then placed against an upright board covered with shiny plastic. Here the initiate was held and bright light focused on him. The entrant then crept into a huge cardboard box and people pounded on the outside of it. The initiate escaped from the din to a convoluted tunnel which led to a chamber in the center of the room underneath a tower formed by a scaffolding. The guest then went out an opening which led to the room proper and was free outside the structure. All went through the maze until it was my turn. Then the crowd, including guests, shouted, "Sacrifice, sacrifice!" They held me against the wall, put me in the cave, and handed me up to the top of the tower. The whole room then broke into joyous dancing. The emotional result was tremendous exuberance and an awe which was frightening to some, for we had really participated in the "mysteries"!

Kerenyi describes a similar ceremony in an Indonesian dance symbolizing the first murder—the murder of the maiden Hainuwele, who had done many good deeds—and the springing of life of all types from the parts of the victim's body after burial. In the dance, the maiden is "danced" underground by a human labyrinth which winds closer and closer to her until she is pushed into a pit in the middle. Then the dancers do a stamping dance symbolizing her burial and the stamping of the earth over her. The myth says:

> . . . only after Hainuwele's murder could men die and only then could they be born again. At the end of the mythologem the Indonesian Kore [a Kore is maiden, mother, lover all in one] appears, who now becomes the Queen of Hades — the Kore Satene. She was the youngest fruit of the first banana tree, and ruled over the first men while yet they had committed no murder. Because of the murder of Hainuwele she became angry and set up a great gate on one of the nine dancing places; it was the gate of Hell and at the same time the gate to human life. For only those who had passed through the gate to Satene could remain men in the future, but she herself dwelt on the Mountain of Death ever after the first murder, and men had to die to come to her. The killing of Hainuwele was the way to humanity and the dance of death was the dance to birth.[2]

[2] *Ibid.*, p. 187.

We had truly danced the myth through total involvement with ourselves and unself-conscious commitment to the group.

Is not this the significance of the funeral of the great man who "loved somebody"—the recital of the story of a man who was sacrificed because he was good, whose words and deeds (like the parts of Hainuwele's body) were planted all over the earth, and who gave new life to an ideal and to a people through the vitality of these immortal words and deeds. This was the celebration of the way to true humanity and to rebirth through the tragedy of death.

Where were the children at Martin Luther King's funeral? Did we adults forget that they needed to share this tragedy, to be comforted and reassured and not forgotten and ignored at a time like this? Let our children in—let us participate together. Let them grow up and face the tragedy and the hope of mankind. The child as creator needs the sense of being totally involved in himself, his feelings, thoughts, and reactions; but this must expand to an interplay with others and finally lead to collective ritual. The child, to be a creator, must live so that his life and art come together—one source feeding into the other—the life source into the art and art into life. Children must live and experience emotionally the significant events of our society through participation in its symbolic events. Art is symbol and symbol goes deep into the core of society. Herbert Read has said this: "The artistic activity might . . . be described as a crystallization, from the amorphous realm of feeling, of forms that are significant or symbolic. On the basis of this activity a symbolic discourse becomes possible, and religion, philosophy, and science follow as consequent modes of thought."[3] Now is life and now life and art are merging. The child must participate in the now of this amalgam of art and life if he is to become a creator.

[3] Herbert Read, *Icon and Idea* (Cambridge: Harvard University Press, 1955), p. 18.

# 23

# The Child Performing

## by Erika Thimey

Children's theater, when it succeeds, develops total growth; it entertains, educates, stimulates, and provides a distinctive form of emotional experience. Through the process of identification, effective theater has therapeutic value for the performer as well as the spectator. Given such long-term, complex objectives, we succeed in varying degrees. Nevertheless, we must not underestimate the impact a good theater experience can have on young people. This recognition is one of the causes of the rapidly expanding children's theater movement.

Children's music and drama theaters have traditional acceptance; it is more difficult to develop and sustain a good children's dance theater. Yet in my experience with the Dance Theater of Washington, D.C., I have observed that one can reach young children more profoundly through dance than through music or drama. Young children have a keenly developed kinesthetic sense that enables them to respond instinctively to dance.

Every child enjoys movement and play-acting from his toddler years on. A child develops by imitating the people and world around him. When language is still an unmastered skill, movement serves as a main form of expression. Yet each child has a different personality, despite this great desire for imitation. One need only observe several children at play. The uniqueness of each becomes apparent even under the same circumstances and in the same environment.

The young child is not really aware of his body. A great part of early dance training consists of acquainting the pupil with the different parts of his body and exploring their movement ranges and possibilities. At this stage, the child moves and dances spontaneously for personal satisfaction, energy release, and self-expression. It is natural for a child to play and dance alone at first. The ability to cooperate with others comes with maturation. The younger the child, the more the teacher uses play forms as early dance training.

What has play to do with art? John Martin says this:

> In play, aside from its immediate satisfactions, the child learns skills and adaptations, both physical and emotional, which develop enormously his capacity for meeting the problems of practical life. Its values have become so widely recognized that it now finds a place in the formal educational program in all enlightened communities. Similarly, art provides an extension of the emotional potentialities, leading to easier adjustment, larger tolerances, broader visions. When vague and half-felt needs are brought to light and synthetically satisfied for a moment in the imaginative world of art, the first step has been taken on the road to their more realistic satisfaction in life. Thus, though the senses, nerves and muscles have no traffic with morality, their ultimate action in both play and art is to increase the powers and to extend the range of all men's lives.[1]

Theater is an outgoing activity that demands response or the expectation of response. "The actor, or the dancer, does not create his work for the mere pleasure of the process but always with the vision that the work itself, once created, will give back to those who see or hear it, something of what he has put into it. From this vision he derives his satisfaction."[2]

These are some of the reasons the preschooler cannot be a performer in the true theatrical sense. A children's dance theater program can be a traumatic experience when the audience suffers with and for an exposed and frightened child forced to present a memorized "dance number," as in a "recital." I cannot criticize severely enough this practice of presenting preschool and elementary school children in programs for the general public. It amounts to exploitation of the child and is a great disservice to him.

The child needs encouragement to continue the development of his individual gifts and personality. A wisely planned program for schoolmates and parents can serve this purpose well and become a wholesome experience. Practically every child enjoys and benefits from showing off a special skill or mastered trick. A sensitive teacher can lead students to short improvisations which continue to preserve personal involvement and spontaneity even with repetition. Children also benefit from the discipline that such a program necessitates when their inner security is strengthened by it. It is quite wonderful to observe the attending parents' pride—as moving as the absorption of the dancers in their make-believe world. It is marvelous to see the ingenuity, freedom, vitality, and joy the dancers exhibit as they express themselves.

It is a very special moment for a teacher of creative dance when the pupil reaches the phase in his development when he is able to transform his body

---

[1] John Martin, *Introduction to the Dance* (New York: W. W. Norton & Co., 1939), pp. 41-42.
[2] *Ibid.*, pp. 40-41.

into an instrument. Then the body is not merely used instinctively and unconsciously for self-expression or physical exhilaration, but is used consciously with full awareness of its potentials and limitations. Then, as Martha Graham puts it, "movement becomes significant." Now the teacher can really open the door to an immensely rich world for the student—the world of art and theater. I believe that only when a child reaches this phase of awareness can he become a performer in the true sense. Sometimes this happens as early as the pre-teen years, more often at high school age.

Various choreographic and production aspects of theater differ, of course, according to whether the company is composed of professional adults or older children. Usually, older children enjoy performing for younger classes. They feel superior and safe from criticism, which bolsters their ego. I encourage such performances by junior and senior high school students as an exercise in projection and learning to feel one's audience, to communicate.

For teen-agers I am careful to select material and subject matter which is meaningful to the students. They choreograph their own work. I give the older children a choreographic or structural problem to solve. They have the liberty to approach it abstractly or to motivate it with an idea of their own choosing. Once I asked them to move only as a compact mass and a contrasting line. After explaining how a sculptor would deal with this problem, I supplied large blankets and wooden sticks, heavy rope and poles. After much dehumanized exploration, we then dug into the same problem without props, using only the human body. The results were quite amazing, ranging from the sublime to the ridiculous. We combined the best studies into a suite and had an exciting theater piece. We performed it for some younger classes; they were fascinated. One of our most powerful dance studies developed from the theme "Air Pollution." Most of the work was choreographed by the students. It was almost frightening—the fervor and absorption with which the teen-agers took to and identified with such a negative subject. I provided the main outline and framework. Another time we explored space, emphasizing height, which led to studies with mobiles. The students created some very ingenious mobiles and dances, again ranging from the humorous to the profound, from pop art to pure abstract design. I must emphasize, however, that all these studies and dances were developed slowly and undertaken solely to benefit each performer, to help him express his ideas and to improve his technique.

I work very differently with the adult professional company of my Dance Theatre for Children. For financial reasons, time is of utmost importance. The choreography is provided to the dancers complete with all details, phase by phase. Technical inadequacy is not tolerated. Only competent dancers, who are able to learn quickly, are engaged. There is no time for improvisation, experimentation, or change. The entire production is organized and prepared for the benefit of the audience. Every minute of every rehearsal is geared to this

future audience. The dancer is the valuable instrument with which I can express my choreographic ideas. The dancer works hard to understand these
ideas and to project them sincerely through the strength of his personality and
artistry. I have learned the importance of including a talented child dancer,
whenever possible, in the cast of our adult professional productions. A children's audience identifies with the child on the stage. Each time this has also
proved to be an invaluable experience for the child performer, who is supported by the projection and artistry of the adult dancers.

Dance is a wonderful means to bring our cultural past to the child and to
make the present more comprehensible. (Mythology, folklore, figures from
history and literature, music, paintings, sculpture and architecture—all can
be danced.)

With civilization becoming more and more complex, we have to find new
ways of expression and new ways to educate. We have to overcome the great
danger of being isolated and separated in myriad specializations of cultural
and economic deprivation. Only the contemporary arts can reflect our time
as a unit. Therefore, it is of the utmost importance that school children have
the closest possible association with the various contemporary arts, in order
to be fully aware of and to understand the present.

The modern dance is a particularly expressive phenomenon of our time,
since it often combines with other arts—music, poetry, sculpture, and painting. For this reason, modern dance brings to the child the most intense kind
of artistic experience possible. Experience with a children's dance theater offers
a full range of opportunities to participate as performer and as part of a
knowledgeable audience.

# 24

# Education Comes Dancing

## by Evelyn de la Tour

Currently, educators are probing the value of dance as a vital and essential form of human expression. Dance has proved itself not only in theater and movies, on television and the concert stage, but in the places of study and instruction, from preschool to postgraduate. Happily, some educators are consulting the dance profession for help in improving education through dance.

Tragically, educators will be engaged in the same battle as the contemporary dancer. Most parents and children know of dance only what they have seen or heard of its four most popular varieties: ballet, tap, acrobatic, and ballroom. The Yellow Pages in most towns, including the capital of the United States, list more or less (often less) as follows what their dance studios offer: ballet, tap, toe, acrobatics, personality singing, square and folk dancing, ballroom dancing, baton twirling, discotheque dancing, modern jazz, modern dance, and "slimnastics." This is not to question the integrity, standards, or proficiency of the teachers, or the value of the individual courses offered, in these studios, but to support my contention that only the minority have been exposed to the idea that the study of dance could be used as an educational platform. A few educators with vision, courage, and hope are exploring dance as a human language which will further the understanding of the languages of mathematics and science. Dance taught as a springboard for the learning of other subjects will help the student to know his subject with his whole being —mentally, physically, and intuitively. Anna Pavlova is reported to have said, "Life would probably have far more meaning and light if, side by side with the teaching of reading and writing, people were also taught to dance beautifully." This needs to be qualified as regards what it is to "dance beautifully." There are so many kinds of beautiful dancing. Pavlova may have meant that children would be trained to move "beautifully" within the formal and stylized ballet techniques. In her generation, dance instruction was excluded from institutions of academic learning and was regarded as vulgar and immoral. From Pavlova to our American dance pioneers, there has been tremendous change in comprehensive concepts of dance. Yet we as a people do not recognize or reward the magnificent achievements of American dance performers and American dance educators.

Teachers Publishing Corporation (Darien, Connecticut) lists in its 1968–69 catalog over 650 teaching aids, 200 of them *brand new*. The list of curriculum areas included in their index reads as follows: social studies, language arts, music, foreign languages, mathematics, professional aids, science, arts and crafts, and early education. Where is dance? It is certainly not in the schools. It is in the active dancer, so busy performing and teaching that he has no time for verbalizations, for formally recording his personal approach to the teaching of dance, or for analyzing his creative efforts.

In the last twenty years the art of teaching dance has improved to a fantastic degree. It is because of the intense concentration and focus on basic dance elements and the development of dance themes. Development of better dance curricula has not only produced outstanding dance artists but also helped to cultivate a more knowledgeable audience. But who will have the vision and power to overcome Roger Bacon's four stumbling blocks to truth: the influence of fragile and unworthy authority; custom; the imperfection of undisciplined senses; and the concealment of ignorance by the ostentation of seeming wisdom.

While I have been experimenting and exploring educational dance with children, a talented colleague, Maida Withers, has been somewhat paralleling my approach with college students at George Washington University in Washington, D.C. She and I believe that every human being is born to dance. It is our heritage. It has been so throughout the ages, but somewhere in history this truth was covered over by civilization. Bacon's stumbling blocks to truth are greatly responsible for the denial of man's birthright; that is, to live his dance daily. The new dance curriculum should illuminate all of man's daily actions; it should help sensitize him to all of his natural movements. These include the gestures of menial tasks, such as washing dishes or clothes, sweeping floors, getting dressed, eating, straightening out disorder, walking to school, running to catch a bus. All natural actions can be developed into structured rhythmic dance sequences. Natural gestures can be defined as prose. Prose can be beautiful, but when natural gestures are crystallized into dance gestures, they gain a certain magic and become poetry.

I believe that if schools give children little dance tools for little people during their formative years, children will be able to continue using them constructively all their lives. The same dance tools are taught and used with the non-dancer as with the future professional dancer, be he teacher or performer. (I say "professional dancer" rather than "dance artist" because no matter how significant and successful a dance curriculum might be, it cannot produce the artist; a fine or even great craftsman perhaps, but not the artist. The artist is born an artist; the study of dance merely helps him mature, and leads him forth to find his own dance language.) Over a century ago Walt Whitman wrote, "I hear America singing. . . ." I hope American educators take up where Whitman left off and can not only hear America singing, but see America dancing.

I believe the modern child will improve the quality of his life through educational dance. All agree that all art media used creatively improve the quality of our lives; but only the medium of movement, the art of dance, can use the whole of man as the creative tool by which he expresses himself and is therefore able to communicate his uniqueness, to identify himself and realize his relation to other beings, nature, and the universe. For a moving celebration of this wholeness, turn again to Walt Whitman—to his poem "One's-Self I sing"—and, for our context, change the word *sing* to *dance* throughout.

## ONE'S-SELF I SING

One's-Self I sing—a simple, separate Person;
Yet utter the word Democratic, the word *En-masse.*

Of Physiology from top to toe I sing;
Not physiognomy alone, nor brain alone, is worthy for the muse
   —I say the Form complete is worthier far;
The Female equally with the male I sing.

Of Life immense in passion, pulse, and power,
Cheerful—for freest action form'd, under the laws divine,
The Modern Man I sing.

Specifically, what are the dance tools that must be fashioned to a child's size? There are four basic elements of dance: design, dynamics, rhythm, and motivation. Design includes floor patterns; levels (height, depth) and orientations (horizontal, vertical) in space; and linear development of body shapes and gestures—in straight lines, in circles, in over-all architecture filling a given space with more than one figure. Dynamics uses energy which produces certain qualities of movement: to mold, to fly, to float, to radiate. Another use of dynamics relates movement metaphorically to voice: to whisper, to talk softly, to talk in a natural tone, to shout. Rhythm is defined simply as the breaking up of fast and slow intervals, the making of intervals in different tempi. Motivation is a purpose, a reason, an idea or feeling that cannot be expressed in words—the desire to feel the mere joy of jumping, to defy gravity, to move swiftly in space, to create a mood.

I am sometimes asked: What is the difference between the technical dancer and the artist dancer? I can perhaps best answer this question by discussing another: Does the critic use a different set of standards and criteria for judging the child and the adult performer? I believe not. Whether a person is young or mature, it is not mastery of intellectual and physical technique alone that determine the artistic merit of his work. That work, be it a painting, a poem, or a dance, will not be worthy of framing, publishing, or performing on stage unless that most important ingredient has been added—the intuitive experience. It is intuitive involvement of brain and body in the work at hand that produces the organic whole. Imagine that we have two paintings by eight-year-olds. One of them, let us say, has more spontaneity than the other, more freedom, continuity, rhythm. In that one, the artist let the accident take over. That one has the expressive simplicity. Suppose we ask a distinguished art critic to judge these two paintings. Would he use a different set of standards, different criteria, than he would use in judging the work of a well-known painter? Again, it all depends on the point of view. Was the reason for painting to communicate a definite idea? If so, was the artist—child or adult —successful? Certainly the critic is not going to compare the child's graphic technique with that of the adult. Technique in any medium needs years in which to develop. But technical ability is the tool developed through intense, persistent work, not the essence of imagination and intuition. The criteria and standards for judging the creative distinction of intuitive work remain constant.

I believe that everyone is born with a complete set of intuitions. Remember when working in some subject became fun? You felt rewarded by achieving a finished painting, a piece of sculpture, a story, a poem, or a dance. Surely the experience is memorable because of the intuitive elements, not because of mere intellectual and physical endeavors. Somehow, when we achieve something intuitively it becomes our own. It fulfills the basic needs of our being— the need of having an identity, the need of being heard, the need of proclaiming our uniqueness, the need of functioning effectively as part of an environment. All this can come about only when we find our intuitive way through the technical complexities of learning processes, whether in art or academe.

# The Contributors

IRMGARD BARTENIEFF is president of the Dance Notation Bureau, New York City, and director of its Effort-Shape training program. She studied for three years with Rudolph Laban and has introduced his kinetography to American colleges and dance centers through her lectures and her *Studies in Labanotation*. Mrs. Bartenieff serves as consultant to the Bronx State Hospital (in dance therapy and research) and to the Cantometrics Project at Columbia University.

HARRIET BERG, whose professional training included intensive studies in dance and dance education, has taught in a number of schools and colleges. Currently on leave from Wayne State University, she is Dance Coordinator for the Jewish Community Center, Detroit, director and choreographer for the Young Dancers' Guild and the Festival Dancers, and member of the Michigan State Council for the Arts.

BONNIE BIRD, formerly a member of Martha Graham's company and a principal teacher in her studio, has subsequently founded and directed dance and theater companies of her own, including that of the 92nd Street YM-YWHA, in New York City, and the award-winning Merry-Go-Rounders. She has also taught in many colleges and universities, and is a board member of the Committee on Research in Dance and of the National Dance Guild.

RUTH D. DILLARD, Principal of the Petworth Elementary School in Washington, D.C., was formerly Intermediate Supervisor for the Department of Supervision and Instruction, District of Columbia, and Reading Specialist for the District of Columbia Reading Clinic. Her postgraduate work was done at New York University (M.A.), Bank Street College of Education, and the University of Maryland.

GERALDINE DIMONDSTEIN, a graduate of the Bank Street College of Education, also studied at UCLA (M.A., Ed.D.) and at the Dalcroze School of Music. She served recently as coordinator of the Arts and Humanities Program of the Central Atlantic Regional Educational Laboratory, a project for development of an arts curriculum for young children.

MARTIN HABERMAN, Professor of Education at the University of Wisconsin, Milwaukee, has helped to change American teacher education by developing innovative internship programs in Wisconsin and New Jersey and for national agencies. In his research and writing (most recently in *The Art of Schoolsmanship*) he is concerned with the preparation of people who can succeed in urban schools.

ANN HALPRIN, founder and director of the Dancers' Workshop of San Francisco, has traveled with her company to major festivals throughout Europe. A certain vivid reputation ("beyond even the . . . avant garde") has no doubt been enhanced by her participation in and direction of such projects as underground art movies, a television program produced in Sweden, and college and university "happenings" all over this country.   CAROLYN GOLDSMITH, associate teacher in the Marin Dance Cooperative, San Francisco, assisted in the preparation of Miss Halprin's article.

JUDITH LYNNE HANNA, consultant in dance and the social sciences, has studied ballet, modern, and ethnic dance forms. She was Associate Professor of Research at the American University, Washington, D.C., and Lecturer in African dance at Michigan State University. Two books, *Urban Dynamics in Black Africa* (1969) and *African Dance* (scheduled for 1970 publication), report the field research she conducted in Africa.

JENNY HUNTER directs her own school, Dance West, in San Francisco, and choreographs for the Jenny Hunter Company. In a distinguished career as performer, teacher, and director for schools, colleges, and dance companies, she has also choreographed works on commission from the Stanford University Music Department, the Carmel Bach Festival, and the San Francisco Actors' Workshop.

RHODA KELLOGG, internationally known authority on children's art and a leading nursery-school educator, is the author of several books in these fields. She is a director of the Golden Gate Kindergarten Association in San Francisco and of the Phoebe A. Hearst Preschool Learning Center there.

EVELYN DE LA TOUR has been principal dancer and soloist in the dance companies of Leonide Massine, Jacques Dalcroze, and Ruth St. Denis, and has appeared in her own dance creations in principal cities around the world. She is founder and director of the Georgetown Dance Workshop and head of two school dance departments in McLean, Virginia.

TOBIE GARTH MEISEL has used her dance background, gained in private and college study, to research and coordinate the development of a dance curriculum for the Central Atlantic Regional Educational Laboratory. She has a bachelor's degree in sociology and psychology from Miami University, Oxford, Ohio, and a master's in teaching from The George Washington University, Washington, D.C., and has taught in elementary school. *From Movement to Dance* (1969) was filmed and co-authored by Mrs. Meisel; and her contributions to the literature include recent articles in the *Maryland Teacher* and *Delaware School Journal*.

VIRGINIA MOOMAW is Professor and Director of the Dance Division in the Department of Health, Physical Education and Recreation, University of North Carolina. There she also choreographs theater productions and guides the research efforts of university and community groups. She is chairman of several divisions of AAHPER and editor of its Dance Directory and of *Dance Research and Theses,* Volumes I through IV.

RUTH LOVELL MURRAY is Professor of Physical Education and Coordinator of Dance Activities at Wayne State University. Appointed to the Michigan State Council for the Arts in 1966, she is currently a member of its executive committee. Miss Murray has served as chairman of the Dance Division of AAHPER, and edited the Division's "statement of belief," *Designs for Dance* (1968). Her major contribution to the literature is her book *Dance in Elementary Education* (1963).

NADIA CHILKOVSKY NAHUMCK is director of the Philadelphia Dance Academy and dance advisor to the Department of Public Instruction, Commonwealth of Pennsylvania. In addition to her teaching, writing, and research, she has choreographed works for television, opera, and concert.

FORRESTINE PAULAY, a member of the Faculty of the School of the Arts, New York University, and consultant to the Cantometrics Project of Columbia University's Department of Anthropology, was co-founder of the Effort-Shape training program at the Dance Notation Bureau.

PHILIP H. PHENIX (B.D., Ph.D.) is Professor of Philosophy and Education at Teachers College, Columbia University. One of his special professional interests is the theory of knowledge, and he is also known to a wider public as the author of *Intelligible Religion, Man and His Becoming,* and *Realms of Meaning.*

MARTHA NORMAN RASHID (Ph.D.) is Professor of Education at The George Washington University in Washington, D.C., where her teaching specialties are research methods and child development. She serves as consultant in early childhood education to a number of state, regional, and national government groups and projects, including the evaluation and research program for Headstart.

PATRICIA A. ROWE is Chairman of the Dance Program and of the Master's Program in Creative Arts in the School of Education, New York University, and chairman of the Committee on Research in Dance. Dr. Rowe has studied with Doris Humphrey, José Limón, Martha Graham, and Hanya Holm. She is the author of articles on various aspects of choreography.

BETTY J. ROWEN (Ed.D.) is Associate Professor, Early Childhood Education, Newark State College, New Jersey. Many of her publications, including her book *Learning through Movement* (1963), reflect a special interest in aspects of dance and creativity in teaching. Her film *Developing Aesthetic Concepts through Movement* is an outstanding recent addition to the educational media.

WILLIAM SCHUMAN is past president of the Lincoln Center for the Performing Arts and of the Juilliard School of Music. Among his distinguished composi-tions, which have earned him a First Pulitzer Prize for Music, are several for dance works choreographed by Anthony Tudor and Martha Graham.

NANCY W. SMITH (M.A., Ph.D.), Chairman of the Dance Curriculum in the School of Music, and director of the Dance Theatre, at Florida State University, was editor of AAHPER's *FOCUS on Dance IV,* and has served as national editor and chairman of the association's Dance Division. She studied with Louis Horst and Doris Humphrey and at the Martha Graham School of Contemporary Dance.

ERIKA THIMEY is founder and director of the Dance Theater Studios in Wash-ington, D.C., and of the Dance Theater, Washington's only professional tour-ing dance company and one of the country's few professional dance theaters for children. Her background has included performance with the Dessau Civic Theatre and Opera, and direction of motion choir works, including hundreds of dancers, for outdoor festivals in Chicago.

GENE C. WENNER, formerly Fine Arts Advisor, Department of Public Instruc-tion, Commonwealth of Pennsylvania, will soon join the staff of the Arts and Humanities Program of the U. S. Office of Education. His background, in music and music education, has included performance and direction for distinguished musical and theatrical groups.

ELIZABETH WILSON (M.Ed., Ed.D.) is Director of Supervision and Curricu-lum Development, Montgomery County Public Schools, Maryland. Her ex-perience has included teaching and administration in many capacities both here and abroad. Her publications deal with various aspects of curriculum and instruction, including the effects of computer technology on education.